EDUCATION
IS NOT ROCKET
SCIENCE

By

Harry Young

This is a work of creative nonfiction. While all the stories in this book are true, some names and identifying details have been changed to protect the privacy of the people involved.

CONTENTS

FOREWORD

Little did he know then that the experiences he had as a young boy in a Welsh mining village in the 1940s would shape his whole life.

It was a life where the local environment was his world, providing rich experiences covering every aspect and requiring practical solutions, only found by trial and error with his school friends.

His laboratory for investigation was row upon row of back lanes behind terraced houses precariously balanced on the steep hillside, and the streams that flowed from the mountaintop before they were polluted by the waste coal duff from the mine lower down the valley, with its gigantic winding wheels.

All this is summed up in his first book, *Valley Boy*, recently published and available on Amazon, and this second book naturally follows on.

This was the starting point for his future life in a profession he holds so dear, and that went on to occupy the next 70 years of his life and occupies his mind even more in these increasingly turbulent times in Education.

He feels that his early formative days in the Welsh mining valley provided the bedrock of his philosophy of Education, which now has even more relevance in this world of mind-boggling reliance on IT for the teaching of children everywhere.

Playing with his home-made tree branch sling and a worn out rubber inner tube in the 1940s-50s — this was his initiation into true "activity learning".

Sling practice picture

CHAPTER 1

It doesn't have to work to be successful

It all started when I was a fresh-faced trainee in 1961. It was the autumn term and I had just started a month-long teaching practice in a secondary school in the Gwent Valley, north of Newport in Monmouthshire.

I was allotted to the teacher with responsibility for Science to start me on my way, as this was one of my study areas. I was given one day's observation as preparation. At the end of the first day the teacher took me aside and said, "Tomorrow I would like you to attempt a lesson on Floatation."

It was an all-boys class of 14- to 15-year-olds. I was, to say the least, terrified!

He handed me a silver foil milk bottle top and said, "This is your visual aid." 'Viz. Aid' – this was the educational term for visual aid in the day. "If possible," he said, "collect some magazine pictures of large oceangoing vessels to use in the lesson tomorrow."

Of course then, in 1961, as there was no internet I couldn't go back to college that evening and look up sailing craft, download pictures and print them off. Preparation was a little more time consuming!

The class teacher did, however, run through the scientific reasoning for this, along with the formula, in order that I was aux fait with it.

Density = mass/volume
(see Glossary for further explanation).

The next day arrived all too quickly and there I was, confronted with a class of boys who didn't look much younger than me at the time. This, added to my absolute terror of being confronted by 25-30 young teenagers, was almost overwhelming.

"This is Mr Young, everyone, and he will be with us for the next month or so. Today he will be giving a lesson on Floatation."

I took a great swallow and started.

I had already set up at the front of the class a large, round, glass-sided vessel, much like an ordinary bowl used in a kitchen, filled to about three inches from the top with water...

Out of my briefcase I produced a milk top (the silver foil cap from a milk bottle) and with all eyes upon me I gently placed it on the surface of the water. My first science lesson was about to start.

Floating milk tops

I posed my first question. "What do you notice?" I confidently said.

Hands shot up immediately and one eager lad said, "It's a milk top, Sir, floating on the water."

A little ripple of laughter travelled around the class. "Of course," I confidently replied, "but why is it floating?"

Immediately the hands shot up again and clearly a lot of them thought I needed help with what appeared to be a really silly question.

5

'It's very light, Sir, and everybody knows that light things float and heavy things sink!"

The young teenagers in the class were beginning to think this young trainee teacher had completely lost the plot.

Now I felt was my chance to establish myself as a young science teacher. "Watch very carefully," I said, as I carefully picked up the milk top from the surface of the water, establishing with everyone that it was the same milk top that had been floating patiently.

I flattened the milk top in the palm of my hand and then folded it and flattened it again. I placed it on the water, but this time I expected it to immediately sink to the bottom, as it was now a solid mass of metal much denser than water.

Instead it remained on the surface!!!!

Inside I was in complete shock. It was supposed to sink. However, the class had not realised what was meant to happen, so I quickly took a second milk top out of my briefcase, never expecting to use it of course, just as a backup, proceeded quickly with the same routine of flattening it and said, "Watch," again, placing it on the surface of the water. That floated too!

I took a third milk top out of my bag and repeated the same routine, this time propelling the milk top into the water hoping that would do the trick, but again, the same outcome and the milk top bobbed back up onto the surface of the water.

Looking up, I saw the class teacher with a little wry smile on his face coming to the front of the class. He said, "Excuse me, Mr Young," taking one of the little flotillas from the surface of the water and placed it on the floor. With the heel of his shoe, rotating his foot, he completely flattened the milk top.

I was filled with embarrassment, with every turn of his shoe. He picked up the milk top and placed it on the water. It sank to the immediate cheers of everyone in the class. All remaining air had been removed, transforming this milk top into a truly solid piece of metal foil.

"Carry on, Mr Young," he said.

Shaken, but realising my schoolboy error, I continued.

The children could now see that the milk top was a solid mass of metal with all trapped air removed, but I still was given a little opportunity to salvage something from this shipwreck!

I showed them a series of pictures of sailing craft of all sorts and posed the question again, saying that these vessels were made of heavy materials yet they floated, and reminded them of what they had said at the beginning of the lesson – that light things floated and heavy things sank.

Through further questioning they began to understand that they floated because the trapped air inside these heavy vessels made them buoyant.

From my point of view I had failed, but in actual fact the children may have learnt more from my failure than if it had gone completely to plan.

The worry of failure should an investigation go wrong and the lack of time and resources to set up practical first-hand investigations, is sadly why a great number of teachers shy away from practical approaches.

The computer simulations on the whiteboards in today's classrooms never fail but do they only result in "short term" memory slots, not fully understood and very easily forgotten!

CHAPTER 2

I hear I forget, I see I remember,
I do I understand

It was 1964 and after three years and numerous teaching practices in varying schools, as well as learning the theory of teaching, it was time to apply for a position in a school.

I had left it very late to apply anywhere but as it happened fate took a hand in the proceedings. A number of my student colleagues had already applied and secured their first teaching position. One of them, knowing that I did not have a position to go to, said that his new head was looking to appoint someone to teach Science throughout the school. It was a small "all boys" secondary school of only three hundred children in the dockland area of Newport S. Wales.

I was invited to go for an interview. What I didn't know was that there had already been three or four teachers in post there the previous year, but all had left for a variety of reasons.

What was in my favour, however, was that my other main subject besides Science in Teacher Training College was Physical Education, at which I was considered fairly capable and that could prove helpful.

The head explained that as the sole Science teacher I would have full responsibility for the subject throughout the school, culminating in the top class sitting the Newport

Certification of Education for Science and if successful, this would be a passport for them to gain an apprenticeship in a number of engineering firms in the area.

The interview was short and then the head produced a series of Science textbooks: 1 to 4, one for each of the four year groups, progressing in difficulty. I was quite excited, though, because while liking Physical Education very much, I strongly preferred being a participant than a teacher of the subject.

Picture of Science Text Books

Additionally, I was given the opportunity to take the top class for Rugby as well as an evening youth club position in charge of Gymnastics and PE at the school. This would immediately give me "street cred" in this single-sex, all-boys secondary school and might therefore help me to be more readily accepted!

At the time I also played for Cross Keys, a top Monmouthshire Rugby Club, who had fixtures against the likes of Cardiff and Newport as well as London Welsh, considered at that time to be one of the best Rugby Union sides in Great Britain, and so I featured fairly often in the *South Wales Argus*, the local newspaper, and later on I was chosen to play against the famous Barbarians during their annual Easter Rugby Tour of Wales in 1966.

Pictures of Rugby teams and club programmes from the time

Cross Keys rugby team. Back row (left to right): Gwyn Regan, Brian Powell, Geoff Catley, Bernard Smithson, John Anthony, Sid Jefferies. Centre: Del Haines, Bob Morgan, Cliff Williams (captain), Roger Beese, Robert Lewis. Front row: Harry Young, David Viney, Alan Talbot, Allan Lewis.

THE LONDON WELSH
RUGBY FOOTBALL CLUB
FOUNDED BY THE LATE DR. T. J. PRYCE JENKINS IN 1885

★

LONDON WELSH

v.

CROSS KEYS

24th OCTOBER 1964

★

OLD DEER PARK, KEW ROAD, RICHMOND

ADMISSION — Ground 2/- (Stand 2/- extra, Enclosure 1/- extra). Cars 1/- each

---

LONDON WELSH v. CROSS KEYS

Saturday, 24th October, 1964 — Kick-off 3.0 p.m.

LONDON WELSH (Colours—Red)	POSITION	CROSS KEYS (Colours—Black and White)
1. H. J. Davies † (Capt.)	Full Back	1. R. Moore
2. G. N. Dwyer	Right Wing	2. R. Beese
3. J. Dawes †	Right Centre	3. G. Musto
4. A. Williams	Left Centre	4. R. Lewis or D. Haines
5. G. Richards	Left Wing	5. H. Young
6. F. Bevan	Fly Half	6. A. Lewis
7. B. Williams	Scrum Half	7. C. Williams
8. T. Davies	Front Row	8. B. Smithson
9. G. Roberts		9. A. Talbot
10. D. Bowen		10. P. Evans
11. D. I. Jones	Second Row	11. G. Catley
12. W. Matthews		12. R. Charlton
13. H. Williams	Back Row	13.
14. G. Davies		14. B. Powell
15. J. Ryan		15. M. Edwards

Referee : Mr. G. W. Polley, L.S.R.F.U.R.　　　† International.

RESULT —　　G　　T　　Pts.　　　　G　　T　　Pts.

PENARTH v. BARBARIANS

15.	A. RAYER	Full Back	J. G. WILCOX	15.
			Headingly and England	
14.	H. YOUNG	Right Wing	W. R. HUNTER	14.
			C.I.Y.M.S. and Ireland	
13.	B. EVANS (Capt.)	Right Centre	F. BRESNIHAN	13.
			U.C.D. and Ireland	
12.	P. JOHN	Left Centre	M. K. FLYNN	12.
			Wanderers and Ireland	
11.	S. WILLIAMS	Left Wing	McF. HATHORN	11.
			Edinburgh Wanderers	
10.	A. WILDING	Inside Half	J. F. FINLAN	10.
			Moseley	
9.	H. JONES	Outside Half	S. J. S. CLARKE	9.
			Blackheath and England	
		Forwards		
1.	F. WILSON		A. B. CARMICHAEL	1.
			West of Scotland	
2.	B. DAVIES		J. V. PULLIN	2.
			Bristol and England	
3.	D. HURFORD		S. JACKSON	3.
			Oxbridge	
4.	E. DAVIES		P. T. C. KING	4.
			Blackheath	
5.	D. BURROWS		J. T. LARTER	5.
			R.A.F.	
6.	P. WALSH		C. W. THORBURN	6.
			Guys Hospital	
8.	L. TOYE		P. J. BELL	8.
			Blackheath	
7.	T. SMITH		T. P. BEDFORD	7.
			Oxford Uni. and S. Africa	

Referee: D. G. WALTERS

PENARTH RUGBY FOOTBALL CLUB
ATHLETIC FIELD, PENARTH
Telephone: PENARTH 58402

OFFICIAL

PROGRAMME

PRICE THREEPENCE

PENARTH v. BARBARIANS
GOOD FRIDAY, 8th APRIL, 1966

Rugby pundits, who during the season have forecast the "tanking" of Penarth in our annual Barbarian game, have had their theory shattered by the recent results. To lose to Cardiff by a mere 11 points and to unluckily lose to Ebbw Vale by 1 point does in many ways belie their forecasts.

Thus we look forward to a good open fast game with the assurance that Penarth will give nothing away and which our now becoming known back row will have plenty to do.

The visit is made more welcome by the fact that "Hughie" has made such progress after a very serious illness that he hopes to be with us once again. A record one should think, hardly a miss since he played against us in 1912.

Will our patrons note that we play at home at 11 a.m. on Easter Monday against Cross Keys. If my memory serves me our last home Easter Monday was against Blackheath for whose visit we had to thank. "The President."

Our thanks are once more accorded to the Glamorgan County Cricket Club for the loan of seating and to Mr. Larry Roberts for the perfect condition of the ground.

Mr Dunn, the head teacher, had been an ex-army captain in the past and was a strong, but fair disciplinarian. The teaching staff of the school and the whole community in this area was very supportive, especially I suppose as they didn't want to lose yet another Science teacher in such a short period of time!

It is no way intended to be disrespectful but over 60 years ago life and discipline in schools was very different and indeed so was society. Discipline at the school was strong but fair and those who transgressed knew what to expect. However, one very hilarious practice comes to mind from that time.

Being a Roman Catholic Sec School, Mr Dunn was known as "Papa Dunn" and Eddie Curran, the deputy head, was known as "Edward the Confessor", for reasons that will become clear in a moment.

They both worked very much as a team regarding discipline. I recall on one of many occasions when the mallet from the full size wooden effigy of Joseph, the carpenter, outside the school hall, had been taken and hidden. Eddie Curran was always given the responsibility of seeking out the offender for this misdemeanour and other offences.

He always did this in a very kindly way by putting his arm around the suspected lad's shoulder, securing a confession out of him, hence his nickname!

Once done the mood would change and he would be sent to Mr Dunn's office, where punishment was administered.

They were the American TV detectives "Hayle and Pace" of the 70/80s.

One nasty guy, one nice guy!

Most of the children's names were "Mac" this or "Mac" that. Macallister and Macabe were just two surnames I well remember, but by far the toughest of the lot was Poretta. His father owned the largest scrap-metal yard in the dockland area at the time. He was as tough as they come and none of the other lads messed with him, including me!

I loved every minute of being in that school and my exam successes in terms of gaining apprenticeships for the boys in the top class improved year on year. Once the syllabus was completed and the results were in, free lessons abounded, allowing them to play football on the tarmac area outside the school gates.

No posh playing fields for games either. I, with other members of staff, had to take them over to the "Rec" (playing fields over the other side of the famous transporter bridge), still working today, as I understand.

There were no changing rooms either so they changed on the playing fields themselves, putting their clothing under the hedge so as not to get wet!

While I settled in to the post well, from time to time the head would drop in on lessons to see how I was getting on and also because he had a particular interest and past knowledge of teaching Science himself.

On one particular day he came in unannounced, to observe me teaching a lesson on pulleys and how they enabled heavy loads to be lifted easily. One piece of apparatus acquired for my teaching purposes a term or so after my arrival, "after I had proved I could stay the course", was a giant practical kit, from a Norwegian company, containing bits and pieces of scientific apparatus allowing me to demonstrate to the children various aspects of Science.

On this particular day I had set up at the front of the class, on the elevated teacher's desk in the Science laboratory, a system comprising four pulleys in order to demonstrate to the boys that using multiple pulleys, heavy loads could be lifted more easily.

Using the four-pulley system I intended teaching the lads that a load four times the effort needed could be lifted. This was established by using a force meter, an instrument with a giant calibrated spring. The 1kg weight could be raised when on the force meter the scale only registered 250g needed, so in actual fact 1kg could be raised by an effort of only ¼kg.

While the children had a grasp of Mechanical Advantage (MA = Load/Effort – for further explanation see Glossary) they didn't exactly fully understand the theory behind it…

Mr Dunn stepped forward from the back of the class where he had been observing and said, "Excuse me, Mr Young."

He called a lad from the back of the class to come forward and handed him a felt pen. "Go to the apparatus, my boy, and put a mark on the string where it leaves the top pulley."

He then summoned a second lad to take a metre ruler and place it in a vertical position directly under the weight, while the other was told to walk away, holding the string taut in his hand.

When the weight had been lifted one metre Mr Dunn called to the boy with the end of the pulley string to stop.

Picture of 4 pulley system

Another lad was now summoned out to take a metre tape and measure how much string had been pulled off the pulley. The length was 4 metres!

The boys in the class were now able to see that while using a four-pulley system would require only a quarter of the effort to raise the load, it would be spread over four times the distance that the load was raised.

This is known as Velocity Ratio. Velocity Ratio = Distance travelled by effort/Distance travelled by load (see Glossary for further explanation).

The principle is exactly the same for gears on a bike... To go up a hill you change to a lower gear but you have to pedal much faster, covering more distance with much less effort! I.e. you go further, but it is easier!!

The boys cheered and stamped the floor in appreciation...

Mr Dunn turned to me and said, "And that's how you do it, my boy!"

The pupils had actually taken part in the investigation, albeit in a limited way with only a few actually getting involved, but now had a clearer understanding of pulley systems and their working.

"I do, I understand."

Sadly while extremely useful, all too frequently demos were still the only avenue to practical work for youngsters. Something I will deal with later in this book.

My time teaching in the secondary sector was all too short and I missed it for a very long period of time, but it was time to move on as my future wife could not play rugby and getting a teaching job in that part of Wales was difficult. More importantly, however, was the fact that we needed somewhere to live!

CHAPTER 3

Making it real and relevant

With all new chapters of my teaching career and life came fresh challenges. It was now the late sixties. I was married and needed teaching positions for both my wife and myself!

As I have already said, securing a first teaching post for my wife was very difficult, so the obvious move was to cross "Offa's Dyke" to the old enemy, the English. I am making this comment with tongue in cheek as this intense rivalry only occurred once a year when it came to playing England at "Twickers" or the "Arms Park" as they were known respectively in those days!

So many of my compatriots were already living and teaching over the border anyway, as the Welsh are well known as a land of rugby players and singers and teachers.

To return to the story, I already had a very good friend from back home, now a teacher himself, with his wife also in the profession in Wiltshire. At the time local authorities there were offering teaching positions and council accommodation to people such as us, to come and teach over the border.

My new wife was immediately offered a position in an extremely large infant school of 300 children on a large council estate in Swindon. I on the other hand was offered a position partly in a secondary school teaching Physical Education and in charge of a youth club on a 60:40 ratio.

While sounding attractive, I really did not want to return to my other specialist subject as I could not see myself enjoying the role of a PE teacher in later life! I politely refused this post as I wanted to fully be part of a school staff. As a result, I was offered an alternative post in a junior school of 500 children, on the same campus site as my wife!

It was ideal, but there was a fly in the ointment. Up until this time I had almost entirely been operating as a secondary school Science teacher!

However, such was the diversity of my teaching qualifications, it allowed me the luxury of transferring to primary education if the need or desire arose.

Fate again took a hand, as it had done when I started teaching years before. The position in this junior school was not to be turned down, as who knew what career opportunities might result from it?

It was a very short summer break as Swindon schools returned sooner in the autumn than schools in Gwent.

I was given a class of 40 children all aged 10-11 in the third stream of a large council estate school.

Picture of me with my first class

There were no 40-minute Science lessons, now all subjects of the junior school curriculum, all day and every day, with 40 children of widely differing abilities and needs! It was a shock to the system!! To say that I found it a struggle is somewhat of an understatement, but with guidance and support from more experienced members of staff I very slowly started to get grips with the situation.

From the very start, however, it was helpful that as a Physical Education specialist I was easily able to engage with the pupils quickly, as all children love physical activity at this age.

Very shortly I ran the school football team. Rugby was almost unheard of in English primary schools at the time. I followed this with the introduction of gymnastics, leading to me entering a school team to complete in gymnastic competitions at high school level. Other responsibilities soon followed, taking over Cycling Proficiency and athletics throughout the school.

Swindon, where I taught, had 23 primary schools at the time with Pinehurst, my school, being one of the largest. Each year we entered the town sports at under 9 and 11 levels.

Football team

Athletics team

Cycling proficiency

Gymnastics team

It wasn't long before we won the under 9 and under 11 shields for the best school, and this continued year after year, very much to the annoyance of the other schools.

All the while, however, I was also concentrating on my classroom teaching skills at primary level, especially at catering for the needs of the individual child. Here, again, the head teacher himself was a great believer in developing the whole child through the "holistic" approach, especially as the school was in a very deprived area with few amenities.

He started to introduce to the staff the benefits of taking children out of the immediate school environment to explore the world around them, widening their horizons. He could see that many aspects of my experience as a Science teacher could help with using the outside world to enthuse children by making learning more appropriate to life.

He developed a strategy that ran parallel to his very structured approach to teaching of the 3 Rs, where these basic skills could be used to investigate the real world and real-life situations outside the confines of the school.

Fund-raising events were organised by the "Friends of the School Association" and very soon a minibus was acquired by the parents for the school's use. It was a long-retired ambulance sold off by the NHS. Proudly along one side we had painted "Pinehurst Junior School".

Below is a picture of the minibus on its way to a 16th-century manor house as part of a history project.

Picture of Mini bus

A list of potential educational visits was drawn up to take all the classes in turn on daily adventures and on return write, sketch, and explore, enabling follow-up work to be thoroughly enjoyable. They were the drivers of what was recalled from their own observations, and more importantly this encouraged them to find out more, adding to their development.

This approach evolved over several years, with me being promoted in the school until I achieved the position of deputy head, when only seven years previously I had arrived as an assistant teacher!

On a personal front I still maintained my interest in rugby and I had represented Dorset and Wilts in the English County Rugby Championships, allowing me to play against players from the leading teams of Bath, Northampton, and Sale to name a few. My rugby career by this time, however, was coming to an end and with two young children I needed to pursue my career aspirations in Education by applying for a Headship at a school of my own, but where would I apply?

Although happy, my wife and I did not want our own two boys brought up in what was rapidly becoming a "London commuter/dormitory route".

Going back to the Welsh Valleys, now rapidly decaying after the mine closure, was not an option and then there it was in the *Times Educational Supplement.*

"Wanted: a new Head Teacher for this soon to be purpose built Community Primary School" in the heart of Powys, Mid Wales.

CHAPTER 4

Opening a new purpose-built
community school

It was November 1979 and having seen the advertisement in the *Times Educational Supplement* I immediately spoke to my head. I had held the position of deputy for 7 years and he agreed entirely that I was ready for a further challenge.

I set to work, filled out the application and within a few weeks I received a letter saying that I had been put on a short list for the position, and that a formal interview for the role of head teacher would take place early in the New Year.

I set to work deciding how to approach the interview and was given a book to read by my head entitled *Getting a Primary Headship* written by twelve former head teachers!

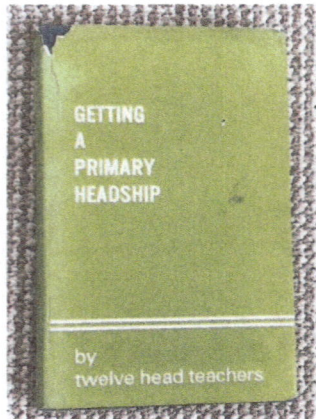

Picture of Book

As we had our own young family of pre-school-age boys, it was exactly the right time to seek a new challenge and place to live, and also to put down roots for the children.

Just as in my first teaching position, fate took a hand and the possibility of securing a headship in such an idyllic rural setting was really exciting, especially as it would be a brand-new, purpose-built community school created by the closure of four small primaries.

As my wife was originally from the area and still had her parents living locally, during our annual Christmas visit we went to see where the new school was to be built. It was to be sited in a village called Garth, approximately six miles from Builth Wells and equidistant from the schools that were to be closed, but there was nothing to see really as only the foundations existed!

We returned to Wiltshire after the Christmas break and there waiting for me was a letter informing me that the headship interview would be on January 12th.

With my carefully rehearsed answers to possible questions I turned up at the County Hall at 9am for an "all day" interview. There were six shortlisted applicants. Of course being a "Young" I was the last of the six to be seen.

At the end of the morning session of interviews a Senior Education Adviser emerged from the interview chamber and said that the afternoon sessions would now only involve three candidates, and I was one of them. The other three were thanked for their attendance, but at that point left.

The odds were getting shorter. I felt the tension mounting as my wife and I dearly wanted to bring up our children in a rural setting, away from the increasingly urbanised area in which we lived.

It was my turn.

"Mr Young, the committee will see you now!"

Further questions arose from all quarters and gradually I had the feeling that maybe, just maybe, I might be in with a real chance!

Now came the final question:

"If appointed, would you consider living in an ex-forestry-commission house… out a little bit in the countryside?"

In fact the village consisted of one row of houses with the backdrop on thousands of conifer trees and nothing else except for a village post office!

What should I say? I dearly wanted the position, however to move from a very large town of over two hundred thousand people was not quite what my wife and I had in mind. I explained that I didn't think this would be fair on my wife with one- and three-year-old children to look after, as she would feel too isolated.

There was a slight pause and an acknowledgement that it was a fair comment to make and then the chairman stood up and said: "Mr Young, we would very much like to offer you this position… Do you accept?"

I had arrived, after 16 years in teaching, now head teacher of a brand-new school.

I was immediately handed the plans of the new school, enclosed in a long cardboard tube.

Picture of me and school plan outside County Hall

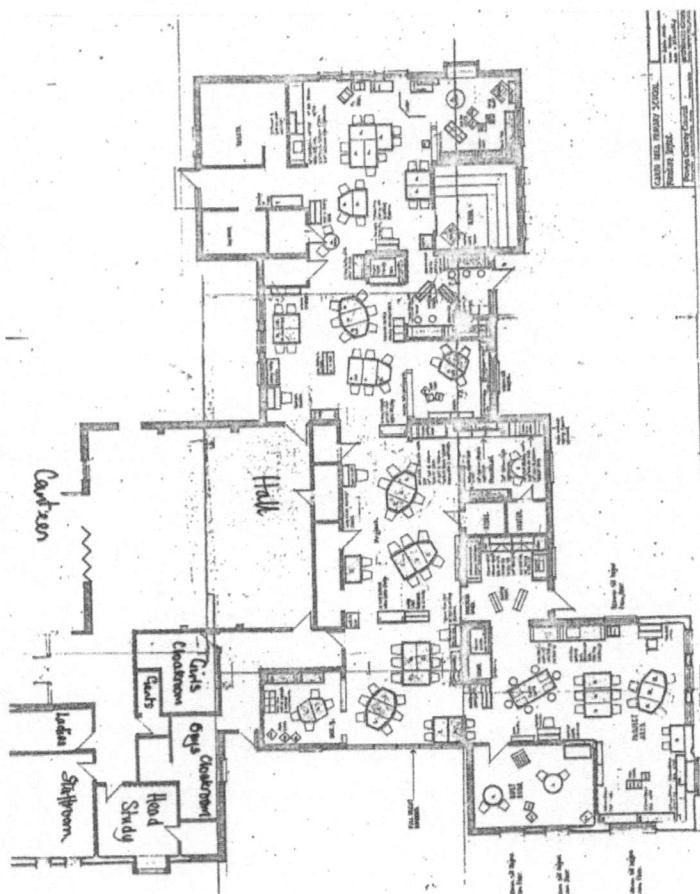

Plan of Internal layout of school

I cannot adequately relate the joy of finally achieving my goal and I left County Hall barely controlling my excitement.

The first stop was to find an empty public phone box so I could phone my wife, as there were no mobile phones then!

The next two months were a blur!! …Where would we live? Would we be able to sell our bungalow in Swindon quickly?

It was now Saturday January 26th and traditionally the weather closes in, especially in rural areas, at this time. We bundled the two boys into the car, making our way to rural Powys… No major roads in Wales in those days!

The first stop was the local estate agents. Nothing for sale in Builth Wells at all and only one property in an outlying village that was described as having a very large back garden, only to find it was almost vertical and impossible to use!

Then out of the blue the following week, after returning to Swindon, we had a phone call to say one property had become available in Builth Wells as a sales contract had suddenly fallen through.

We moved in on Easter Saturday, March 30th, selling our bungalow after only two days on the market as Swindon was a rapidly growing town at the time.

Before I left my former school I was sent on a headship course to a place called Ferry-side in Wiltshire. There were a number of HMIs present and I was given advice from all quarters about how I should proceed. What was clear to me, however, was that the initial strategy and planning would require great consideration and would define how this new school would establish itself.

I was told after being successful in the interview that my new staff would comprise the four former heads of the schools about to close!! This, to say the least, added a little to my apprehension of opening this school and while I had a clear vision of what I wanted to achieve, co-operation and listening would have to be at the heart of this. Especially so, with this unique staffing situation.

I took up my position after the Easter break and for the whole of the summer term, as the school was finally being completed, I visited each of the closing schools for one day every week, gaining an insight into the procedures and methods pursued, with the final day of the week spent with the architects and builders involved in constructing the new school.

Each of the schools had its own character, with staff and children equally diverse.

I had a temporary base in Beulah Primary School as acting head there, just a few miles up the road from Garth where the new school was to be sited. The sitting head of that school had been seconded for a year to Swansea University to achieve further qualifications.

All schools have special, larger-than-life characters and one of those staff members at Beulah was the cook. After lunch on a Friday afternoon she would lean out of her canteen's serving hatch and call out, "How many children have we had this week for lunch?" The paperwork and dinner money had to tally!

Clearly in very small schools, in some cases barely 20 on roll, doing the accounts was not something that would be problematic, but was a vital task that had to be done and the Nursery Assistant as well as myself found this weekly ritual very amusing!

It brought to mind how this contrasted with my former school of 500 children with 16 classes, in many cases 40 or more on roll in each. Each Friday lunch time, the head delegated to me the responsibility of taking hundreds of pounds of weekly dinner money, in small change in money bags, to be banked. It would not be fair or safe to expect the school Secretary to carry bags of heavy coins!

Second on my list of schools to be visited was Llanafan Primary School. It was not without its surprises either! Set on a very quiet back road from Garth to the village of Newbridge-on-Wye, Mrs Miriam Jones, the school cook, always immaculately dressed, was consistently looking out of the canteen window each time I arrived.

During one of my weekly visits there I was talking to the children in their classroom when there was a ringing sound. I looked around the room but could not see any sign of a telephone and the head teacher had temporarily disappeared. The children looked equally puzzled so clearly a phone ringing was not a regular occurrence.

It was left to me...

I looked everywhere for any sign of a telephone cable, eventually deciding that I had found it. Now, where was the telephone?

The cable seemed to take a random path around the room so I picked it up it and hand over hand followed it to the end of the room, then through a little hole in a partition separating another teaching area, across that room, eventually leading to another door, this time with a padlock.

By now, without realising it I had a line of inquisitive children behind me just like the Pied Piper, carrying the cable with the ringing representing the haunting tune played by the flute. The phone eventually stopped ringing.

The head now appeared and I related the story. With a large key in her hand she unlocked the door. It was a small cupboard with a little shelf and a telephone!

Picture of telephone incident

She explained that the Youth Club had access to the school on certain evenings and the phone had to be locked away to stop it being used unofficially by the Young Farmers Club members!

Next on the list was Llangammarch Primary School. This was the largest of the four schools to be closed and was on the main street of the village, with 20-30 children on roll, comprising one infant and one junior class.

I remember well my first visit there. I was almost mobbed. As soon as I entered the main door the children deserted their classes en masse and took me to the stream behind the school where many of them spent their evenings fishing for trout in the River Cammarch, which ran behind the houses through the village.

They were a lively lot and I think I must have been the first male teacher they had ever seen!

Eventually the two teachers there managed to round them up and herd them back inside, and we all ended up in the school hall with the children sitting around me on the floor.

Never say what you are capable of doing unless completely confident about it! In my interview I indicated that I could play the piano and before I knew what was happening I was taken to the piano and asked by one of the teachers to play something for the children.

At least I had told the truth, as I could play but not that well. In my former school the Head came to me one day and said, "Next term, Mr Young, you will have to play the piano for all the school assemblies," as the teacher in charge would be going into hospital and would not be back for a full term!

The last time I had played the piano was when I was in school myself. There was no protesting though as I was the deputy and that was that!! Each weekend I had to practise because the following week, with 500 children and staff sitting around the hall, I could not afford to falter.

This time with such a small group around me I felt even more nervous.

I sat down, all eyes upon me… I did play, but it was quite a nerve-racking experience.

The last school of the four to be visited was Garth School in the small village of Garth itself, and only a few hundred yards away from where the new school was being built.

I always remember entering the old school with its highly polished wooden floors and a hanging pendulum wall clock looking equally proud, with its perfectly rhythmical beat as the seconds passed.

Picture of Garth classroom with children in rows

The children sat in rows with barely a sound except the occasional hand up and, "Please, Mrs Williams…"

Mrs Williams was trained just after World War 2 and was the ultimate professional.

I knew immediately I was in the presence of a very capable professional. She became the Deputy Head, which was a privilege for me. She was the most loyal and dedicated colleague that I have ever worked with. She drove a little grey Morris Minor car every day from her home in Llangammarch Wells, only a few miles up the road. We struck up an immediate professional relationship. She always called me Mr

Young and I reciprocated by calling her Mrs Williams. We never had a cross word.

The following months were a blur…

All sorts of decisions had to be made including equipment for the school and most importantly the teaching structure, in terms of individual class organisation.

I consulted on a daily basis with each of the school staff as to what they felt would be best for the new school, knowing full well, however, that the only workable solution would be a four-class structure with two age groups in each class. I purposefully did not show my hand as I wanted everyone to be part of this new venture.

Next came my vision of how the pupils' educational needs would be best met. All four schools had a proud tradition of establishing a firm foundation in the basics for each child. Clearly this should continue and flourish but in addition, what I had in mind came from my overwhelming desire to see that the children should use their firmly established basics towards the study of the humanities – i.e. History, Geography, etc. – not only from text books but outside the school using the wonderful local environment. Unlike Pinehurst, my former school situated on a deprived city council estate of prefab houses, only intended to be temporary housing after the Second World War but still standing.

Additionally, this would enable each child, I felt, to develop their basic skills further and take ownership of their world in a very creative way, placing each one of them at the centre of their learning.

Clearly while children from the small schools were taken out on visits, hitherto they had not been part of the overall plan to widen their horizons. One reason for this I suppose could have been that in very small schools, a wide age range makes it very difficult to plan meaningful experiences for all.

I felt at the time, however, in my first two terms as the new head, this further ideology was best not exposed to individual staff, but gradually introduced when the school opened to avoid uncertainty and concern about the new head "throwing the baby out of the bath with the water".

While concentrating on the school itself it was also vital to take into account the wishes of individual village communities, who quite rightly might view the newcomer with suspicion. All the small schools had wished for the new school to be built in their own community, but quite rightly the only sensible and viable option was to build it as equidistantly as possible between all four. Additionally, a brand-new name had to be decided.

A questionnaire was sent to parents regarding the new school name in May 1980, while I was at Beulah School. Those consulted were given the option of five different names, with two being in Welsh. The final overwhelming decision was to name the school Irfon Valley County Primary School.

Picture of Questionnaire re school name

I contacted companies about a school logo. It was agreed that a rising sun in a valley would be most appropriate. This was agreed by everyone to exactly capture the feeling of adventure that would unfold for this new school, with me at the helm over the coming two decades.

Picture of School logo

Central to my philosophy was to build cohesion as soon as possible, establishing a new identity with which everyone – children, parents, and the teaching staff – could identify.

To my aid came the well-known School Prayer, of which there are many versions, all with the same aim of unity and starting:

This is our school
May all here live happily together
Let love dwell here among us every day
Love for one another
Love of all people everywhere
And love of life itself
Let us remember that
As many hands build a house
So many hearts can make a school

The school opened on the Monday after the bank holiday at the end of August. It was September 3rd. The official grand opening for the school, however, was to be exactly six weeks and three days from the first day of the autumn term.

I had already decided in advance how this should be approached. There needed to be a form of entertainment for the assembled gathering, to which all children could contribute.

During my visits to the small schools in the summer term I had noted that each had its own identity, with children excelling at various aspects of learning. Two of the schools in particular had dedicated time to teaching the recorder and the children there were quite skillful, while in another more emphasis was given to singing. In this sense the "opening of the New School" had ready-made opportunities for me to capitalise upon. All that was required was a format for me to put it into practice…

The obvious solution was to write a play entitled "Opening A New School". I set to work. One child in particular from year six was ideal to take the main part.

The idea was that the assembled gathering of parents, county councillors, HMIs and the Director of Education would be entertained by all pupils.

On the allotted day, October 8th at 2pm, the scene was set. I welcomed everyone and then as planned there was a knock on the entrance door to the school hall. A young person asked if she could speak to the head teacher, as she was sent by her editor of the Brecon and Radnor newspaper to report on the official opening of the school.

Picture of Reporter in School Hall

The head teacher (myself) told her that entertainment was being provided by the children for the guests.

Each item was introduced by a chosen pupil from the former schools and was in the form of singing, instrumental items, and country dancing.

EDUCATION IS NOT ROCKET SCIENCE

Picture of Programme of Entertainment

IRFON VALLEY C.P. SCHOOL

OFFICIAL OPENING

PROGRAMME OF ITEMS BY THE CHILDREN

1. INTRODUCTION

2. IF YOU'RE HAPPY   ACTION SONG - EVERYONE

3. MISS POLLY   ACTION SONG - NURSERY/
                                                RECEPTION

4. RECORDER GROUP   JUNIOR

5. COUNTRY DANCE   JUNIOR

6. THE THREE BEARS   ACTION SONG - MIDDLE UPPER/
                                                INFANT

7. ONE POTATO, TWO POTATO   ACTION SONG - SOLO

8. STAND UP, CLAP HANDS   HYMN - EVERYONE

LOCAL EDUCATION AUTHORITY

CHAIRMEN

Councillor B. G. Pritchard
    Chairman, Education Committee
    Chairman, Finance and General Purposes Sub-Committee

Councillor Lt-Col J. D. Stephenson, M.B.E.
    Vice-Chairman, Education Committee
    Chairman, Further Education and Community Services
    Sub-Committee

Councillor W. D. Lewe
    Chairman, Schools Sub-Committee

Councillor J. C. Deakins
    Chairman, Sites and Buildings Sub-Committee

Councillor T. F. Thomas
    Chairman, Special Services Sub-Committee

Councillor T. G. Davies
    Chairman, Governing Body, Irfon Valley C.P. School

OFFICERS

T. F. G. Young
    Chief Executive

R. W. Bevan
    Director of Education

P. Wharton
    County Architect

S. V. Woodhouse
    County Treasurer

PROGRAMME

Chairman: County Councillor B. G. Pritchard

1. Opening Prayer and Dedication of the school by the
   Reverend A. Thomas.

2. Unveiling of the plaque and Official Opening by
   County Councillor T. G. Davies, Chairman, School
   Governors.

3. Items by the pupils. (See overleaf)

4. The Director of Education, Mr. Robert W. Bevan.

5. Vote of thanks - Proposed by County Councillor
       J. T. H. Davies, School Governor

    Seconded by Mrs. A. Morgan,
    School Governor

6. Closing Prayer and Benediction by the Reverend D. Evans.

The Chairman of the County Council and Councillor and
Mrs. T. G. Davies will entertain guests to Light
Refreshments at the conclusion of the ceremony when
there will be an opportunity to inspect the school
premises.

43

After 30 minutes or so it concluded, to much applause and appreciation from everyone.

I also congratulated the children, but then pretended to be a little confused and said, "While you have come from four different schools to be at Irfon Valley, whose school is it?!"

One child said, "It's your school, sir, you are the head."

A second child interrupted and said, "No, it's Mrs Lawrence's school, she is the caretaker."

A third child put her hand up and said, "It's Mrs Jones' school. She's the cook and feeds us every day."

After more suggestions I interrupted, and said, "This cannot be correct," and then posed the final question.

"But WHOSE school is it really?"

The very youngest child in the school held up a hand and said, "IT'S OUR SCHOOL!"

Picture of little Girl

We all then sang "Stand Up, Clap Your Hands", and the concert concluded with the children saying the school prayer... Job done!

CHAPTER 5

Planning the Experiences

The school opening was over and had been a tremendous success, with everyone expressing enthusiasm for the inclusive way in which it had been officially opened.

Now, I felt, was the time to start concentrating on my philosophy of using the predominantly rural environment to provide meaningful real-world experiences for the children, identifying a multitude of historical and geographical destinations of interest, something I had helped to develop in my previous school through the "Educational Visits" using the minibus.

Here in my new school, while I did not have the luxury of our own minibus I had the services of Roy Browns Coaches, the local bus company that had the contract for transporting our children to and from school at the end of the day. This was particularly useful as this transport could be used at the start of the day after it had dropped off a number of the children at the school.

Most children travelled to school using a series of small minibuses run by private contractors. The catchment area covered 100 square miles with Irfon Valley C.P. School at the centre of it!

I drew up a list of easily accessible places to visit within the school day so that all children would be able to investigate first hand. I am not suggesting that the children had in any way been deprived educationally, but the area was so rich in opportunity outside the immediate vicinity of the school that it would be almost unforgivable not to capitalise on it.

I hasten to add that, although I shared my overall philosophy with the staff at our regular meetings, I did not foist this approach upon them, but in my role as head and teacher of the year 5/6 class I felt I would be able to demonstrate the obvious advantages of such practices. Hopefully they would be successful with and for the children.

It was clear that the children's ability in the basics was quite sound so the rich historical heritage of the area near at hand in Builth Wells, in the form of the Norman castle built in 1095 after the conquest at the Battle of Hastings in 1066, made this an obvious first choice of investigation. It would involve all subjects of the primary school curriculum and allow the children to use their existing classroom skills for first-hand investigation, putting them directly in charge of their own learning.

I was astonished, however, to find that hardly any of the children had visited the site of the castle or even knew of its existence. I can only suppose because of the small size of the individual schools, visits had not been considered viable for such a wide age range. Each school comprised in most cases only one class of children from 4 to 11 years of age.

In my class of 30-35 year 5/6 children at the time, I introduced them to the idea of producing a plan for investigations during our visit to the historic site of Builth Wells Castle, with prompting them to think about:

1. The history of the castle
2. The geographical importance of its location
3. English/drama related to life in Norman times in Mid Wales
4. Art: Sketching from first-hand observation of what the motte and bailey Norman Castle might have looked like
5. The Science behind the building and protection of Norman castles

But for my first sortie into project work and especially into "practically based" Science in the new school, it needed to be exciting and as practical as I could make it, so all children could engage in learning on a very individual level. They would be the "drivers" of this experience and not the "passengers".

I wanted the emphasis of the visit to be on excitement and enjoyment outside the confines of the school itself, which would be a comparatively new way of working to them.

Preparations were made that included informing the parents, organising packed lunches for those children requiring them, suitable clothing to be worn, and the necessary risk assessment taken into consideration.

Immediately on arrival the scene was set and after the necessary safety talk the children's imaginations were fired with how it would feel to be in a foreign land having to defend yourself from unfriendly locals behind a hastily constructed wooden fortress, and what methods you would use to defend yourself!

They made sketches, took measurements of the castle boundary and sat on the grassy ramparts wondering what these foreign soldiers would have been thinking about coming from a country warmer and drier than Wales!

The visit picture

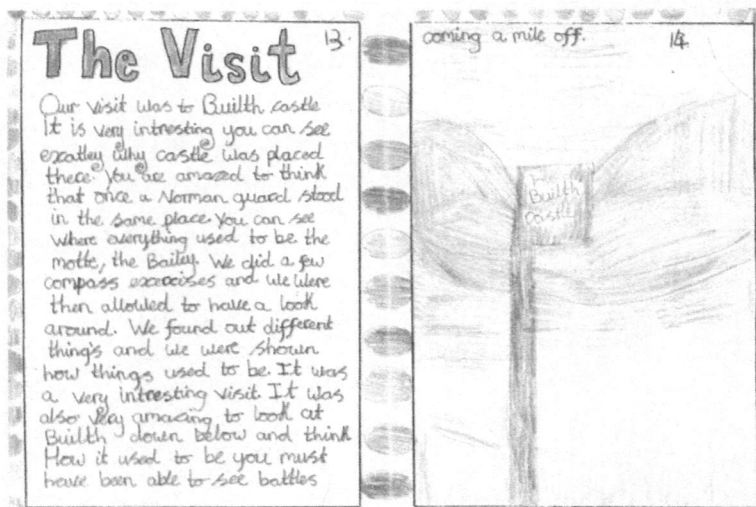

Photo copies of children's write-ups

The children loved every minute of it. We had races up and down the steep grassed banks of the outer castle ramparts and arrived back within the school day thoroughly exhausted but filled with enthusiasm for their newfound freedom and adventure outside the school compound! And with plenty of exciting things to do in school over the following days!

After sourcing historical facts about attacking castles of the 11-12th centuries I challenged the children to make their own siege machines (trebuchets). An array of ancient weapons were constructed from bits and bobs at home in the first instance, I dare say with help from individual dads, including an old tobacco tin in one of the siege engine models.

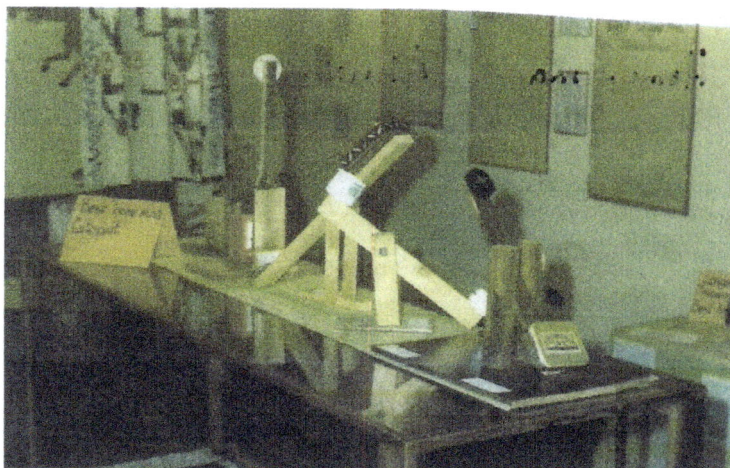

Pictures of "Home- made" attempts of making trebuchets

Back at school we viewed each attempt and promptly set about testing, with the same ammunition for each... a small pebble! It was clear that each one had its individual merits but not one of them could be considered efficient.

All the children, boys and girls, were captured by this newfound freedom of making decisions themselves, and the new possibility of doing things practically in addition to using their basic numeracy and writing skills for a new and exciting adventure. It didn't seem like work now because it was driven by their own enthusiasm.

Using the newly acquired equipment I had ordered from the LEA supply company (comprising lengths of 10mm square wood and round dowel, bench hooks, junior hack saws, sandpaper, and glue guns) the children set to work in pairs making their own siege engines.

Example of Classroom-made Trebuchet

Additional material included empty little plastic milk containers to hold the ammunition (small round pieces of Blu Tack). It was exciting but didn't solve the problem of which was most efficient, as they were all built to the same specification.

To initiate a discussion relating to the idea of mechanical advantage (using a device to make work easier) I refreshed the children's understanding of see-saws, with which they were all familiar. It was clear that a very long throwing arm would be required to propel any missile any great distance.

After further discussion it was also realised that there were two other aspects: the throwing angle and the load used to fire the missile.

Without the children realising it, I had involved them all in the idea of "fair testing" and "design" – two basic strategies in the development of practically based Science.

We concluded, with everyone joining in the investigation making their own estimations, that a throwing angle between 70-80 degrees enabled the missile to be thrown the furthest, and with testing this proved to be correct.

Below are two of the actual write-ups from the children.

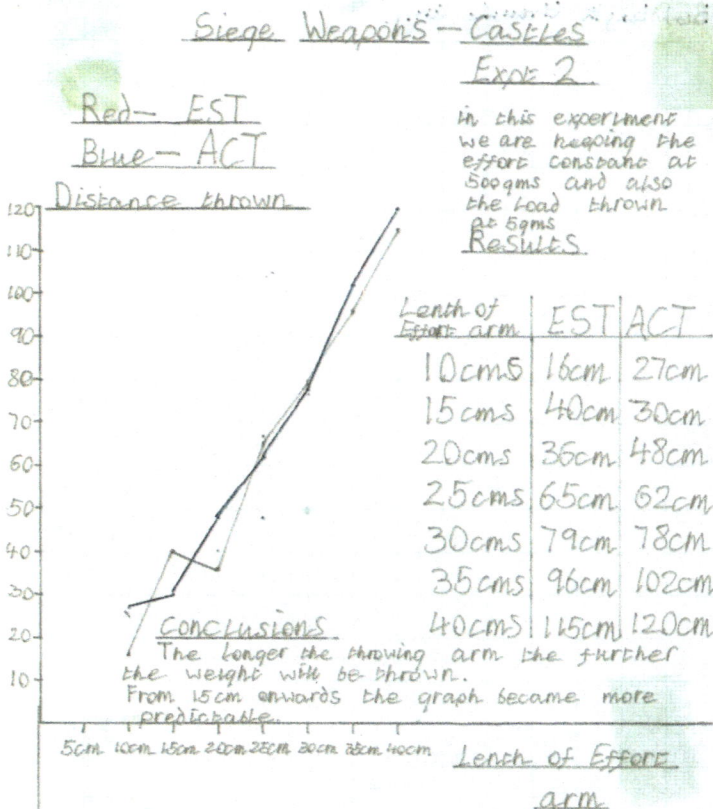

Picture of Length of throwing arm graph/write-up

Siege Weapons — Castles Best
Angle
What we did   Expt 4
On Thursday March 17th class
four done an Experiment with the best Angle
The Catapult which had 8 different lengths
of strings. They were the stopping points.
What happend The results were surprising I was
only right on one. The results were.

20° 0cm
30° 0cm
40° 0cm
50° 0cm
60° 60cm
70° 62cm
80° 102cm
90° 117cm

by A.L.Mills
Conlusions   The best Angles were between
70°90°.

Picture of Throwing Angle graph/write-up

After this success we made a very large model from wood and even enlisted the school cook in charge, Mrs Miriam Jones, to provide us with an empty catering fruit tin so we could fill it with concrete to give the siege machine (trebuchet) throwing power.

Picture of 12th-Century trebuchet

An exhibition of the children's work was put on show in the Local Arts Centre in Builth Wells.

The making of the siege engine had thoroughly grasped the imagination of all the children, and this was followed up with looking at the historical background to the Norman invasion, the building of wooden Norman castles all along the English/Welsh border (The Marches), the geographical significance of why Builth Castle was placed dominating the ford of the River Wye, and the use of contour lines. Using an ordinance survey map of Builth itself the children learnt how to a draw a cross section of the land upon which the castle stood.

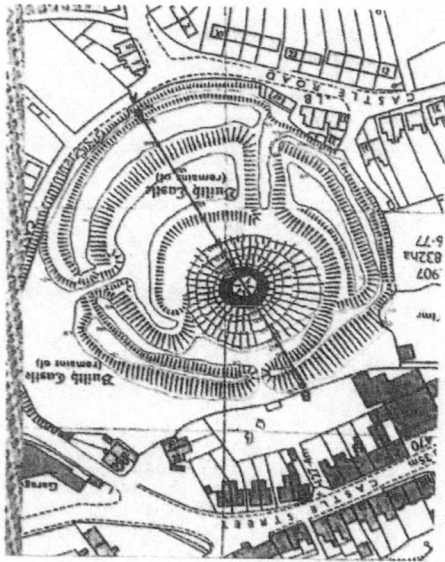

Picture of cross section drawn by one pupil

While the children were only 10/11 years old it seemed to be the natural thing to do and they loved it!

As time progressed and inevitably projects relating to real situations outside the school were repeated, a few years down the line subsequent classes visited other castles in Wales within reasonable travel distance, including the famous 12th-century Norman castle in Caerphilly.

On this occasion children produced their own project folders. Below exemplar work from one: *The Normans Project.*

What is important about all this work is that it trained the children to become self-motivated autonomous learners.

Please note the Table of Contents and Index from one of the children's project folders.

Table of Contents

The Normans

The Normans originally came from Norway and Denmark and were vikings. They came in big long viking boats with dragons' heads carved on them. They settled in northern France and they named it normandy. Charles the 1st let them have the land if they would become christians and fight for the king if he needed them. The King of Frances' nick name was charles the simple. When Edward the confesser died William his cousin was supposed to be the King but Harold became king instead and William was fuming

who were they?

The Invasion

William was afraid to take his army over to England because Harold would be waiting for him on the beach. Tostig was Harolds half brother. William made friends with Tostig to go to the county of England so that William would have more men to defeat Harold. The plan they made was for Tostig to go to the north of England and William to land at Pevencey. William took his army over in ships. Before William set sail it was a late summer gale and some of the ships got damadged. The Normans thought they were going to be protected because the comet was in the sky. William used about 700 ships. They set sail on the night of Sept 27th and they landed on the morning of Sept 28th. They marched to Hastings and set up a fort.

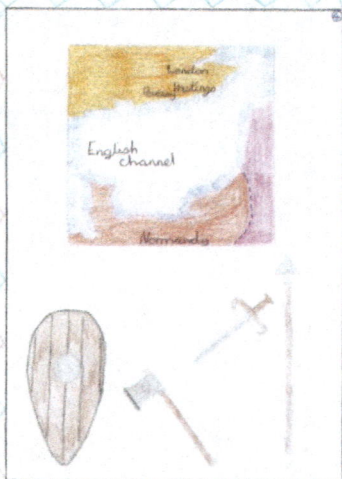

London
Beachy
Hastings

English channel

Normandy

The Battle of Hastings

Harolds army wasn't waiting for the Normans because Harold was fighting Tostig his half brother in the north of England. Harold got the news because his messenger galloped all the way up to tell him Harolds army marched from stamford bridge. The two armies met each other on Oct 14th 1066. The two leaders put their armies on Senlac hill and Telham hill. The first army to attack was the Normans. Williams trick was to run down the hill and Harolds army would follow. The Normans hacked him to death. William marched up to London and on Christmas day William became King of England 1066.

Builth Castle

Builth Castle was first built in 1095. It was a typical motte and bailey castle. The castle was built at Builth Wells because it was a major strong hold of the lordship and guarding an important ford crossing on the river wye. When the castle was rebuilt from the stones from the black quarry near Builth. The master mason was paid 4s and 6½ per week. There are 40 foot soldiers and 9 troopers guarding the castle. In 1691 Builth was burnt down to the ground. The town was rebuilt from the castle.

The Visit

We left school at 1·15 pm. We went in two mini buses. Mr Young took the one and Mr Williams took the other one. When we got there we went over a style on to the castles ground. Mr Young gave us a little talk and then we had 5 minutes to run around. When that 5 minutes was up we went on top of the motte and Mr Williams told us where North, East, South and West was. Then we marked on our maps where A,D,C,D,E,F. We measured from those points all the way around the castle.

To say that this new "project work" strategy had been a success was truly an understatement and other members of staff were keen to follow this approach, finding visits within travelling distance of the school that would provide practical activities, creative writing opportunities, and sketching from "real life" situations for the children in their particular age groups. The list of opportunities was endless.

Each class teacher was encouraged to draw up a list of venues suitable for potential visits with their children's age group. Care was taken that over a period of time projects and associated visits were not repeated until that cohort of children had left their class to proceed to the next.

A complete timetable of projects and visits for the school was compiled so all classes had a balanced programme of investigative opportunities with associated visits for a "Whole-School Approach".

CHAPTER 6

The Whole-School Approach

After the success of the my project with the year 5/6 class, other members of staff were filled with excitement and enthusiasm to be involved with the with their own classes outside the confines of the school.

I sat down to make a list of all possible places of interest within travelling distance that could provide a meaningful experience during the school day, and allow for exciting work involving all subjects back at school to last a number of weeks afterwards, driven by the children themselves.

As time progressed we added to the list, setting certain criteria for places to visit during each of the school terms. One term the emphasis might be on a place of geographical significance, another of historical interest, a third of scientific significance, while a fourth term might concentrate on nature. In this way it would be possible to create balance across the curriculum.

Some work, however, involved bringing the resource into school as well, especially with "People Who Help Us" projects. These involved The Policeman, The Ambulance Paramedic, The Fireman, etc. This was very popular with the infant classes.

The visit of the police with the patrol car was a particular hit and the equipment, including handcuffs and the obligatory police helmet, thoroughly captivated the children.

The following table shows topic plans for the year 5/6 class. Clearly a plan had to be developed to cover a four-year period, so that no staleness or repetition would creep into the children's work or indeed for the teachers.

These projects were all linked to educational visits that undertaken within the school day, resulting in a meaningful experience.

I was very keen, being a former Science Specialist, to focus very much on visits and activities that would bring the children into "First-Hand Practical Activity" mode, where they would be "making, doing and investigating themselves", much as I had done as a child in the Welsh mining village in the 1940s. (See my recently published book, *Valley Boy*, on Amazon.)

Class 4 Topic	Visit	Investigation Focus	Scientific Focus
1. The Normans	Builth Castle	Siege weapons	3 and 4
2. Birds	Gigrin Kite Sanctuary	Bird covering	2
3. Moving on water	Brecon Canal trip	Water transport	3 and 4
4. Bridges	Builth bridges	Bridge construction	3 and 4
5. How we lived 1939-45	Brecon Army Museum	Light investigation	3 and 4
6. Freshwater life	Garth Lake	Aquatic life	2
7. Anglo Saxons	Offa's Dyke, Knighton	House construction	3 and 4

8. The Wind	Bryn Titli Wind Farm	Wind investigation	3 and 4
9. Water	Elan Valley Dams	Water investigation	2, 3, and 4
10 Trees	Local Forestry BWS	Wood investigation	2, 3, and 4
11. How we lived 1939-45	Brecon Army Museum	Light investigation	3 and 4
12. Moving on Land	Llandrindod Cycle Museum	The wheel	3 and 4

With the formal introduction of the National Curriculum in the eighties came the introduction of study areas in relation to Science

Science within the NC (National Curriculum) indicating key focus areas

Sc1: Investigative Procedures

Sc2: Plants/Animals/Humans

Sc3: Materials

Sc4: Physical Processes (e.g. Light, Sound, Electricity)

Having compiled a list of possible visits to give real context to the project/topic, it was necessary to identify possible scientific investigations within each.

The following plans were set out for the year 5/6 class and similar plans were made for the other classes.

1. Nature Science

| Educational Visit | Red Kite Centre (Rhayader) |
| Project/Topic | Birds |

Scientific Investigation   Sc 2. Life Cycle of Birds
                                          Sc 3. Bird Covering

2. Transport

Educational Visit   National Cycle Museum
                                          (Llandrindod Wells)
Project   Moving on land
Scientific Investigation   Sc4 (Development of the
                                          Wheel)

3. Nature Science

Educational Visit   The Elan Valley Dams
                                          18 miles from school
Project   Water
Scientific investigation   Sc3 (Rain Cycle)
                                          Properties of
                                          water/purification

4. Transport Communication

Educational Visit   Builth Wells bridges
                                          6 miles from Builth Wells
                                          Iron Bridge, Telford
                                          (70 miles) Follow-up visit
Project   Bridges
Scientific Investigation   Sc 4 (Bridge Structures)
                                          Sc 3 (Bridge materials)

Irfon Valley C.P. School, 4 Year
Rolling School Project Plan for all four classes

Class 1 1998/1999	Class 2	Class 3	Class 4
1. Trees	Supermarket	Ourselves	The Normans
2. Myself	Ourselves	The Tudors	Birds

64

3. Water	Jobs	EDC (St. Lucia)	Moving on land
1999/2000			
1. Fairy Tales	Colour/Light	The Weather	Bridges
2. Animals	Birds	The Victorians	How we used to live
3. People/Help	Post Office	Mini Beasts	Garth Lake
2000/2001			
1. Colour/Birds	Trees	Food/Farm	Trees
2. Birds	Water	The Victorians	How we used to live 1935-45
3. Transport	Homes	Trees	Movement on water

These projects/topics were selected to give scope for using the local environment.

They were also chosen to give a balance across the Humanities i.e. History/Geography with Science in mind. Not all topics could be driven by an educational visit. Where possible they were included but also were subject to change as the need arose.

In both the junior classes it was necessary to repeat certain projects every two years because of the NC requirements.

In the next chapter, Chapter 7, there will be exemplary work by children from all four classes regarding the individual projects above.

An excellent way of revisiting the "educational visit" back at school was to make a video film during the visit itself. This had a number of advantages in that it not only refreshed the memory of the visit but gave the children an extra dimension of "ownership" by adding their own thoughts while there. Class 4 became particularly adept at this. Each video lasted about 20-25 minutes with each child taking part, adding to their self-awareness and confidence.

Making their own sketches also became a feature of all visits, as seen on the covers of some of the many videos with the following examples.

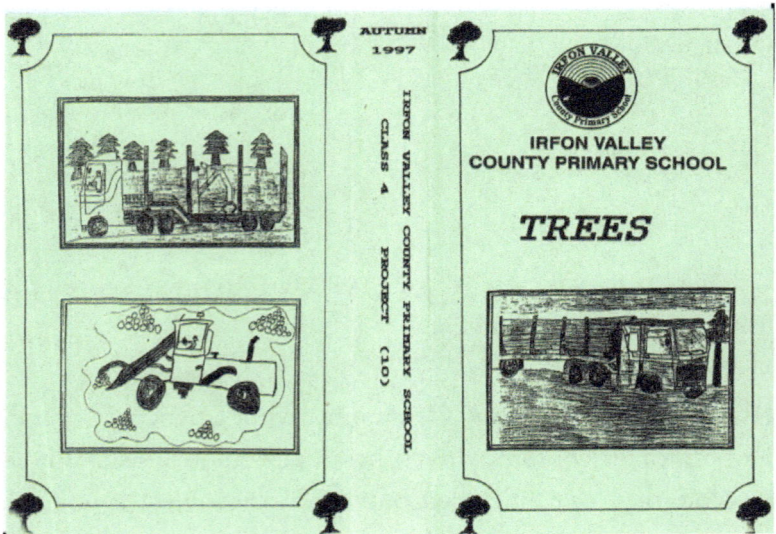

Project: Trees
Venue: Saw Mills at Newbridge-on-Wye

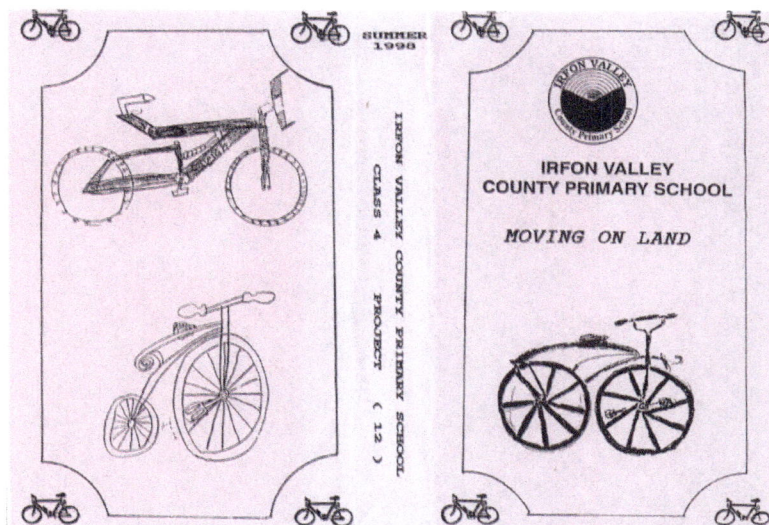

Project: Moving on Land
Venue: National Cycle Museum Llandrindod Wells

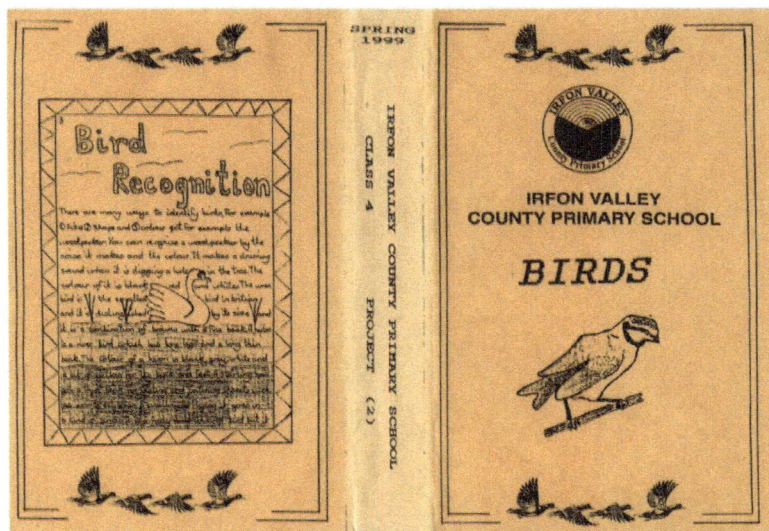

Project: Birds
Venue: Bird Sanctuary at Gigrin Farm Rhayader

Project: *Water*

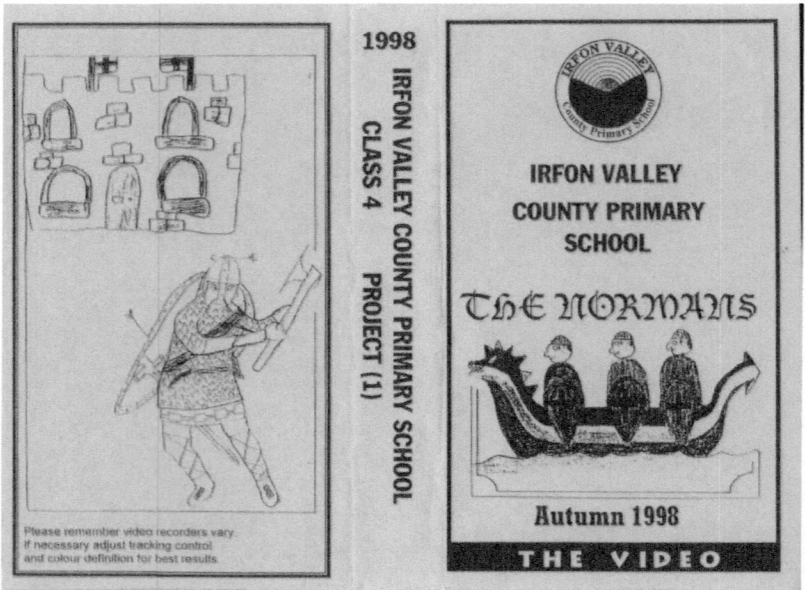

Project: *Normans*

CHAPTER 7

Putting it into Practice

Planning is one thing, but you then have to put it into practice. It was pleasing to see that the staff saw the advantage of making work more alive for the children by using the environment to enrich their learning in a meaningful way.

As already covered in Chapter 6, the introduction of the new National Curriculum in the eighties helped in this respect, as all learning was put into easily distinguishable categories, especially in Science.

It was divided into four distinct areas of learning called Attainment Targets, namely:

Sc1. Scientific Enquiry

Sc.2. Study of plants, animals, and humans

Sc.3. Materials and their uses

Sc.4. Physical Processes through the study of Light, Sound and Electricity

Following each Educational Visit there was always the possibility for the children to undertake a practical investigation. As a result the staff and I developed a series of progressive investigative sheets for each class, increasing in difficulty with older year groups.

Class 1 Pre NC (Nursery/Reception)

Class 2 Key Stage 1 (Yr. 1/2)

Class 3 Key Stage 2 (Yr. 3/4)

Class 4 Key Stage 2 (Yr. 5/6)

Writing Up Investigations

This was not a joy for a lot of children, but is a technique that has to be learnt. The "What I found out" section on the investigation sheets revealed how much the children had learnt.

Representing the information in graphical form was stimulating for children as it gave them the opportunity to make a prediction about what they thought would happen, and then compare it with what actually did happen.

Below is a graph by a year 6 child who found that his predictions got closer as the investigation proceeded into the throwing ability of a Norman siege machine (trebuchet) when attacking a castle.

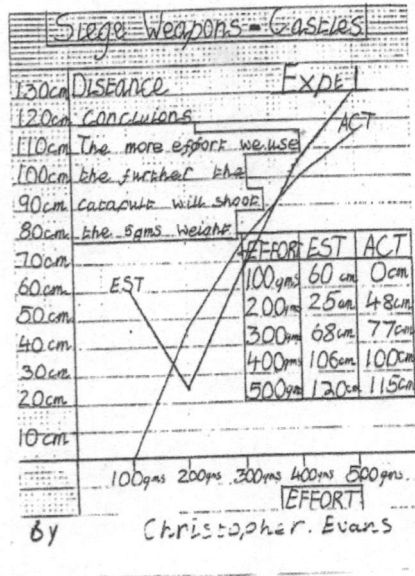

Graph: Trebuchet (1981 pre-National Curriculum!)

The rest of this chapter is given over to actual examples of the practical approach to learning adopted by the school.

Class 2

Topic 2 (1999/2000): Birds

Sc2. Living processes

One of the most exciting and stimulating ways to provide children with direct first-hand experience of living processes is to bring the resource into school. As example of this an incubator was bought for the use of all the classes on a rota basis.

For a little over £100 this resource proved invaluable in the children's understanding of the life cycle of birds.

Obviously this scientific investigation was not "instant" as the whole process took place over a three-week period. We were very lucky that a local lady who bred chickens – Mrs Hall – kindly agreed to bring in eggs for this purpose and give us all guidance regarding the use of the incubator.

Below is a diary of a year 2 child over a three-week period
The diary follows specific events, namely:

Day 1. The arrival of the eggs

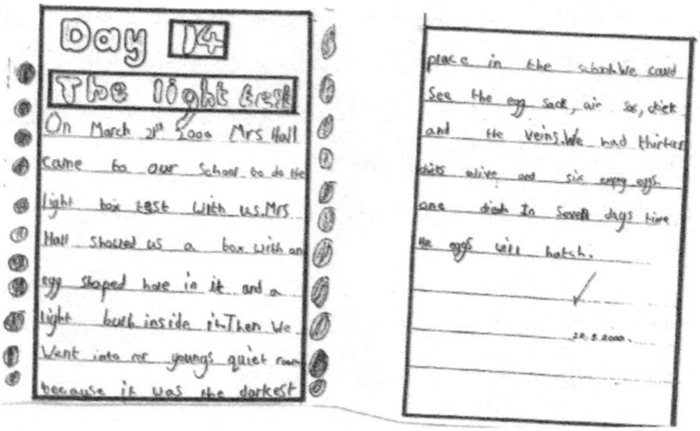

Day 14

The light test

On March 21st 2000 Mrs Hall came to our School to do the light box test with us. Mrs Hall showed us a box with an egg shaped hole in it and a light bulb inside it. Then we went into mr youngs quiet room because it was the darkest place in the school. We could see the egg sack, air sac, chick and the veins. We had thirteen chicks alive and six empty eggs. one died. In seven days time the eggs will hatch.

Day 14. Testing the eggs

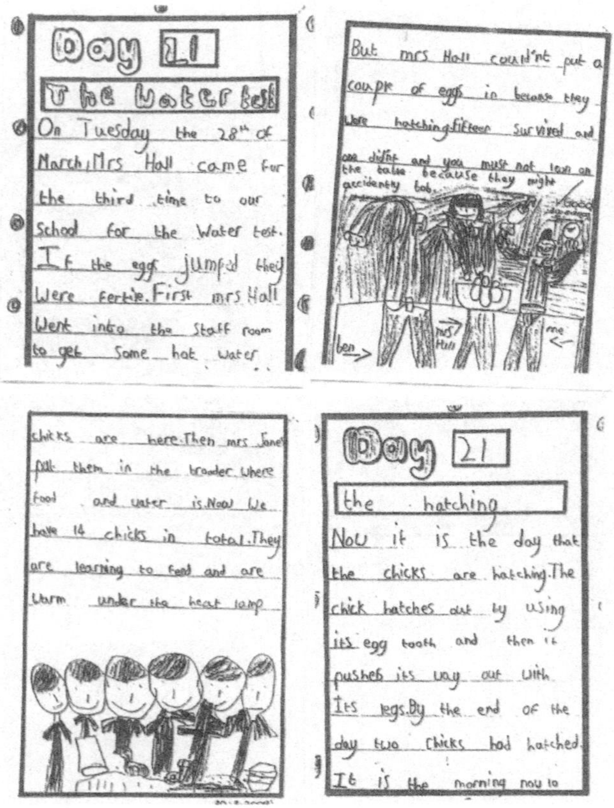

Day 21

The Water test

On Tuesday the 28th of March, Mrs Hall came for the third time to our School for the Water test. If the eggs jumped they were fertile. First mrs Hall went into the Staff room to get some hot water...

But mrs Hall could'nt put a couple of eggs in because they were hatching. fifteen survived and one didn't and you must not lean on the table because they might accidenty fall.

chicks are here. Then mrs Jones put them in the brooder where food and water is. Now we have 14 chicks in total. They are learning to feed and are warm under the heat lamp.

Day 21

the hatching

Now it is the day that the chicks are hatching. The chick hatches out by using its egg tooth and then it pushes its way out with its legs. By the end of the day two chicks had hatched. It is the morning now to

Day 21. The water test/ hatching

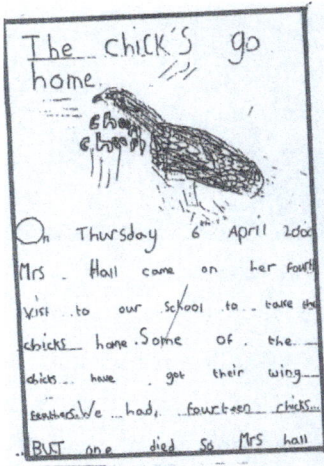

The chick's go home.

On Thursday 6 April 2000 Mrs. Hall came on her fourth visit to our school to take the chicks home. Some of the chicks have got their wing feathers. We had fourteen chicks. BUT one died so Mrs hall

only took 13 back To get the chicks. Mrs Haul took a box with fresh straw and an hot water bottle. The black chicks go to the Small Breds Park and owl center. The genral ones go to the farm at Montrose

✓ Good. 11.4.2000

Day 28. The hatching/chicks going home

Leading on directly from **class 2's** investigation on the **life cycle of chickens** was **class 4's** investigation into **how birds keep warm** in winter and posed the question of whether feathers were really the best for keeping them warm!!

Class 4

Topic 2 (1998/9): Birds

The following one account is from a year 5/6 child.

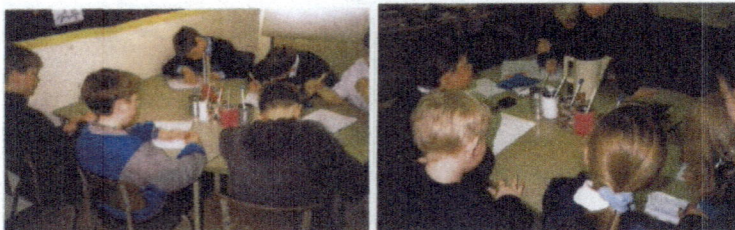

Pictures from the investigation

These pictures show two groups of children investigating the effect of different coverings on tins of hot water, with the tin simulating the body of the bird. Each group had five identical tins, but each one covered in a different material.

From this investigation the children concluded that feathers are the best option for insulation purposes!

It is interesting to note, however, how astute one of the pupils was when he concluded in his prediction that there wouldn't be that much difference in the results, because none of the tins had a lid and therefore a lot of the heat would rise straight out of the tin anyway!!

Take special note of his prediction! He was far more astute than of any of us, including ME!

QUESTION / PROBLEM	The best body heat barrier

PREDICTION / REASONS I dont think there is going to be not much difference between the 5 tins because I reckon that all the hot air will rise out of the top because they havent got lids on.

FAIR TEST RULES ① Same amount of water ② Same size tins
③ Same starting temp ④ Same amount of covering
⑤ Check temp at same time

VARIABLES Type of covering

RESULTS	Tin 1	2	3	4	5	1	2	3	4	5	
0 min	85	85	85	85	85	94	95	95	95	93	
5 min	83	84	82	83	81	80	81	80	80	81	
10 min	77	78	75	77	76	71	72	72	71	72	
15 min	62	63	63	61	64	64	65	65	65	67	
20 min	56	57	57	59	59	58	60	60	59	63	
25 min	51	53	53	52	55	54	55	55	55	57	
	Estimate					Actual					

WHAT WE DID	We covered the tins with tin 1 nothing. Tin 2 paper. Tin 3 corrugated card. Tin 4 bubble wrap and tin 5 feathers. Mr Young filled each tin with the same amount of boiling hot water and we put the thermometers in the tins and we read how much it dropped every 5 minutes

WHAT I/WE FOUND OUT	We found out that the tin with no covering lost the heat in the fastest time. The paper tin, card and bubble wrap lost the heat about the same in the same time. The tin with feathers covering it kept the water the hotest in that amount of time because the hot air got trapped between the layers of feathers.

PROBLEMS	We did not have any problems

DRAWING/DIAGRAM	

Write-up of mangonel experiment

Needless to say we did repeat the investigation with lids this time and had a far more conclusive result.

Associated with the topic of birds, in class 4 a number of local venues were used to enhance the project further.

Below are photographs of the children visiting the mountain centre at Libanus just out of Brecon, to make bird cake and construct bird boxes of their own. Note the sheer enjoyment of the children (spring 1994).

Pictures of Libanus Visit, making bird cake and constructing bird boxes

Another popular visit for the children of year 6, when undertaking a project on birds, was the 1998 Spring Term visit to The Red Kite Centre at Rhayader.

Picture of Yr. 5/6 Visit to Gigrin Farm

Class 3 (Yr. 3/4)

Project 2 (1999/2000) – The Victorians

Meanwhile when studying a project on the **Victorians** children from **class 3 (yr. 3/4)** visited a venue in Presteigne, around 30 miles from school, called "The Judge's Lodging", a Victorian mansion, which introduced them to life in Victorian times.

Back at school they discovered that it was a great time, with the invention of electricity, and the visit provided the stimulus to look at simple electrical circuits and investigate conductive materials.

An investigation by one child

Class 3 (Yr. 3/4)
Topic: The Victorians
Sc.4 Electricity

In the following photographs Natalie and Carys are about to test a block of wood to see if it will conduct electricity, and in the second photograph other children have discovered that copper is a good conductor.

Photographs from the investigation.

Class 4 (Yr. 5/6)
Topic 1 (2000/2001): The Anglo Saxons

Following on from the work in Class 3 with their topic work on the Victorians and electricity (Sc. 4), this set the scene in Class 4, year 5/6, to make **Quiz Boards** to go with any of their projects. In this case consolidating their understanding of electricity.

Basically to make one of these the child would plan one side of a stiff piece of card with a series of questions and possible answers relating to their topic, but the answers on the right-hand side of the card would be in the wrong order.

Paper clips would be placed next to the questions and answers. Plastic-coated wires would be used on the reverse side of the card to connect the questions with the correct answers.

The circuit wires were then concealed by a covering on the back of the card. To test the Quiz Board would require a circuit consisting of a battery, bulb holder, two pieces of electrical wire, and two crocodile clips.

It was a "fun activity" to do and it reinforced the children's understanding of electricity as well as the work on their particular project!

The Quiz Board identified all the towns along "The Marches", a man-made ditch separating King Offa's land in England from the marauding Welsh. We also made an Educational Visit to Knighton where there is an interesting museum devoted to King Offa.

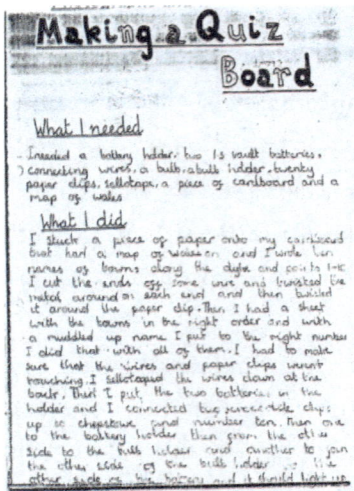

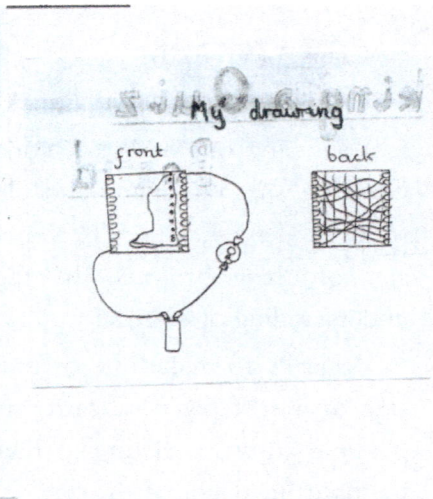

Photographs and write-ups re Quiz boards

Class 3

Topic 3 (1998/1999): St Lucia (EDC)

The National Curriculum for Geography required that all children should study other environments, especially EDC countries (Economically Developing Countries).

By chance a member of staff had links with a school in St Lucia and so there was an exchange in terms of letters, etc., with the children there.

As St Lucia is so far away and separated by so much water, it was decided to undertake experiments regarding water and its buoyancy effects on water transport.

The question posed was why there is a special marking on the side of oceangoing ships called "the plimsoll line". This mark is there to see how much cargo can be put onto the vessel without danger of it sinking.

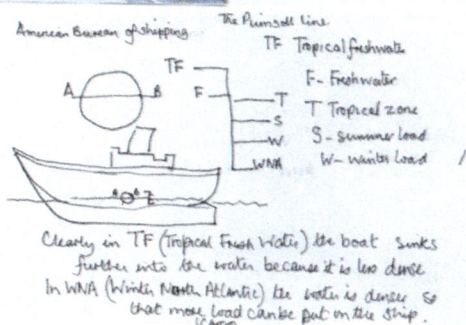

The Plimsoll Line

The children in this experiment are using a piece of wood in a jar of water weighted at the bottom to see how deep in the water it could sit without sinking.

Their experiment was linked to adding salt to the water, to see if this made a difference to how far it sank.

In this photograph the children are measuring the wood's height above water level.

In this photograph the child is measuring out the amount of salt to be added. The experiment started with clear water, then added 20g of salt each time before measuring the effect.

The results and a graph by one of the pupils

Class 2 (Yr. 1/2)

Topic 3 (2000/2001): The Postman

Focus: Sc3 Materials

Meanwhile in class 2, children were conducting investigative work regarding the Post Office, to decide what packing would be safest for a parcel.

Picture of work

Class 2 (Yr. 1/2)

Topic: Materials – The supermarket shopping bag!

Focus: Sc3

In this project the children were finding out which shopping bag would be best to use in wet weather!

Picture of work

Class 2 (Yr. 1/2)

Topic (1999/2000): Colour/Light

Focus: Sc4 Light

A topic on Colour/Light provided a very interesting investigation for year 1/2 children in the autumn of 1999/2000. The following account is by a year 1 child. Note that he predicted the light colour would be best and made the connection to the importance of wearing something light in colour at night!

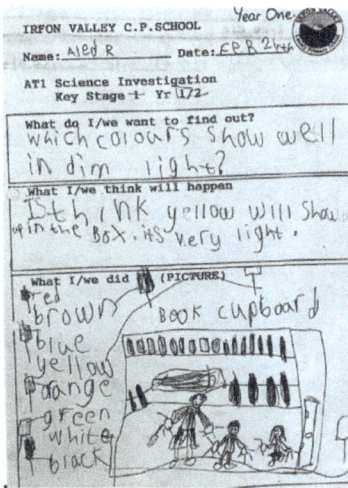

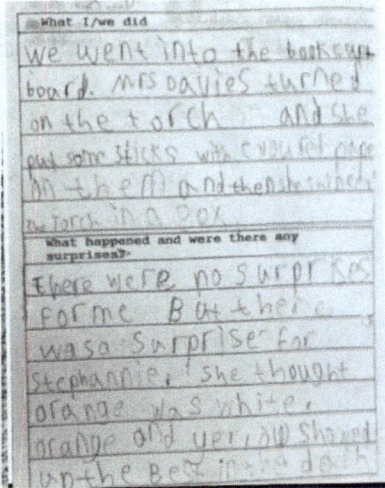

Picture of work

Class 4 (Yr. 5/6)
Topic (1999/2000): Bridges
Focus: Sc3/4

Another excellent topic to undertake as development can be followed from a historical perspective while at the same time provides a very practical avenue for investigations into bridge development over the centuries.

The Builth Wells area is generously provided with bridges, as is most of the county of Powys and also with historians. Armed with this potential, it was easy to pursue this project in a very practical way.

One funny and significant story relates to the bridge leading out of Builth Wells on the Llandovery road. Originally this was a three-stone-arch bridge which stood for 150 years across the River Irfon, but in 1937 it was replaced by a single-arch "Iron Bridge".

The demolition team foreman wanted to take the bridge down in good time, but didn't bank on the near catastrophic accident when he mistakenly told the men to remove the keystone in the centre of the bridge, causing it to come down rather more quickly than he anticipated!

Bridge collapsing picture

Miraculously no-one was hurt and apparently the foreman was given a brand-new Ford motor car for getting the demolition done in record time!!

The children thoroughly enjoyed this project especially as it got them out of class on numerous occasions, with a number of other bridges in the area to survey.

The number of times I heard the children say, "This is better than working," when that is exactly what they were doing.

The climax to this project was a visit to the famous "Iron Bridge" in Telford; the first to be constructed in Great Britain.

The children involved in the project were year 5/6 and took part in a whole series of practical investigations into bridge construction. The first of which was:

"Who can make the strongest bridge out of a single sheet of A4 paper bridging a gap of 20cm?"

The following investigation was the third in a sequence relating to piers, and which shape would be the strongest to support a bridge.

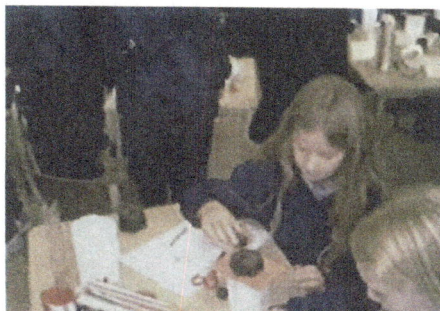

Anwen and Briony are testing the strength of the hexagonal pier. At present it is supporting 1½kg.

Ryan and Dale are testing out a pier with a square cross section. It is holding 1kg.

Bridges..........Problem 3

We have found out that Piers help to make a bridge stronger,but we want to know which pier shape is best?

Apparatus: Bridge piers of different shape (cross section)

Results

PIER SHAPE		EST LOAD	ACT. LOAD	POS.
△	triangle	200gr	300gr	4
▢	square	700gr	1000gr	3
⬡	hexagon	1000gr	1300gr	2
◯	circle	1500gr	2000gr	1

Fair Testing Rules Use the same size paper. 2. Put card ontop, 3. Put weights in middle.

What we did We made piers of four different kinds of shapes as in the results colum. We put weights on the card and tested them to see how much it could take. We also estimated.

What we found out I found out that the circle is alot stronger than I thought because it has a big space around the centre of gravity, making it more stable.

Class 4 (Yr. 5/6)

Topic 1 (1998/1999): The Normans

Finally I return to the practical Science I initiated almost 20 years earlier, and this time instead of the trebuchet initially constructed, the children made their own siege machines called mangonels.

This too was an ancient "throwing machine" for attacking castles but was considerably smaller and more manoeuvrable.

Drawings and actual models the children made using 10mm square lengths of wood, small rectangular three-ply boards for the body, nails, plastic spoons, elastic bands, and ammunition made of 1cm cubes of wood are below, including pictures of the children making and using the siege weapons.

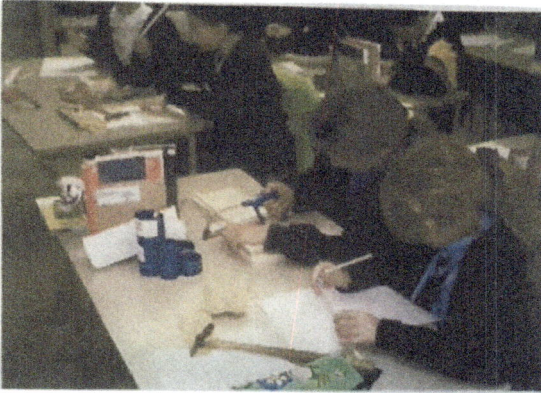

Pictures of mangonel construction

The next picture shows two girls busily making their own mangonels.

Other children busily making their mangonels

The children, boys and girls, thoroughly enjoyed making their own siege weapons and testing them out.

Their ancient "war machines", however, were powered by twisted elastic bands. They found out that more twists of the band resulted in more power, producing a pattern to the distance thrown with increased twists of the band.

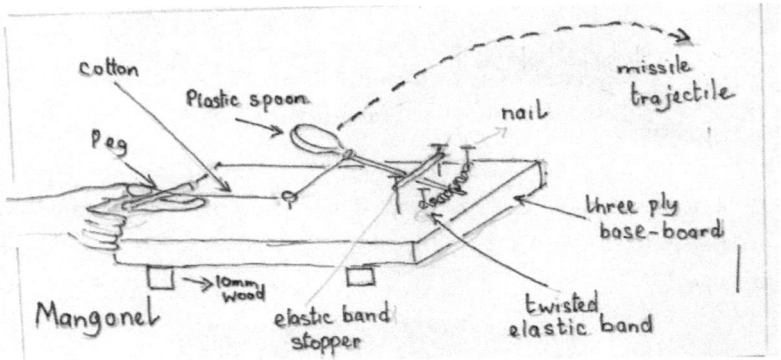

While nine groups of children found this to be the case, three groups found that there was a falloff of efficiency with more turns and Clara, an extremely bright child, told everyone why, in her explanation, as you will see when you read the write-ups below.

The Normans Project Folder

The following pictures are of children in class 4 busily engaged in practical investigative work driven by their own enthusiasm. They are oblivious to the photographs taken and completely absorbed in the work.

Class 4 pictures of practical work

Topic Work

Each topic individual classes took part in was interwoven with the "basics" (Numeracy and Literacy) that all children were involved in each day, but the role of the project, which included in most cases an educational visit, was to enhance this work, to allow the children to develop in their own way, putting them in charge of their own learning.

Each folder combines the Humanities of Geography and History in a very meaningful way, enabling the children to have a greater awareness of the rich heritage of their own environment.

The project approach introduced at Irfon Valley, I believe, also helped the children to be independent learners, a very valuable skill at secondary school and beyond.

CHAPTER 8

The Importance of Display

There is no better way of raising a child's confidence level than to display his/her own work for everyone to observe, and to create a feeling of well-being. This also needs to be shared on a wider level with the parents, and an excellent way to do this is by holding exhibitions of the children's work on such days as open evenings.

At Irfon Valley these were twice yearly, one during the autumn term and the second near the end of the school year. Not only did they serve as an opportunity for the parents to discuss their children's work concerns, if any, at the start of the year, but to discuss the progress made by each one of them at the close of the academic year.

This display covered a cross section of work accomplished by each of the individual classes during the year, and was set up in the school hall along with individual class videos made for the second open evening in June, after the end-of-year reports were sent home to parents.

The school hall was split into four specific areas for each class to display work from the autumn/winter, spring and summer terms.

The following examples come from class 4 (yr. 5/6).

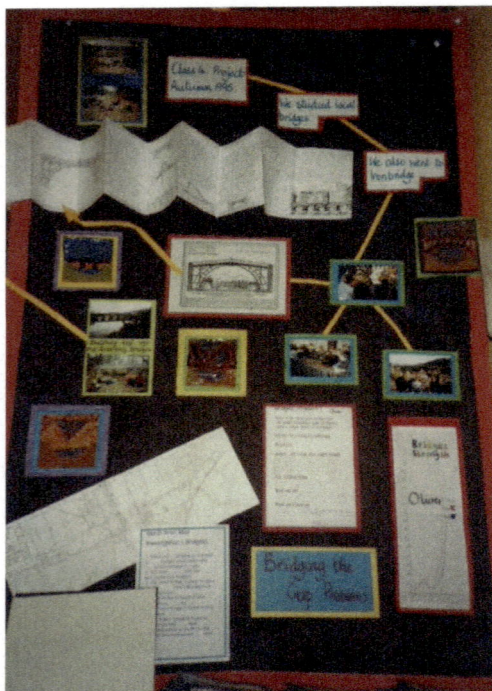

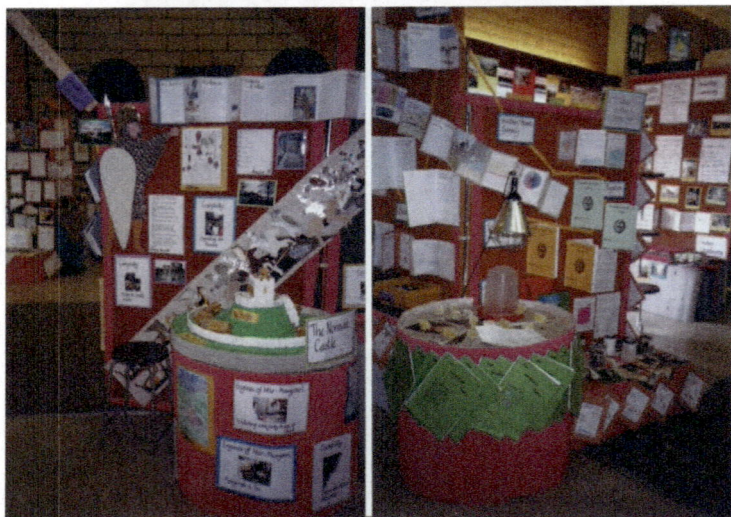

Pictures of displays in the hall

Making video films (mentioned in Chapter 7) relating to their projects and class visits in the surrounding locality served as a reminder of their visits, to drive forward further work during the school term.

During open days parents were treated to showings of these videos in the school hall while also looking around at individual and class contributions.

A few funny incidents occurred at this time when discussing the year's work of the children with individual parents. One such incident that I'm sure I can be forgiven for repeating related to a lad called Keith Lawrence. While discussing Keith's progress during the year with his mother I said, "I must thank you, Mrs Lawrence, for listening to Keith read every night and signing his reading record book."

Mrs Lawrence said, "What reading record book are you referring to, Mr Young? I haven't seen any reading record book."

Next morning Keith came into class and I said, "Keith Lawrence, please come out, I want to talk to you! You have been telling porky pies, haven't you!"

Keith was one of the best, most powerfully built props I have ever had in the school rugby team and he was a very happy-go-lucky lad, always with a smile on his face, but reading was not a joy for him, as it wasn't for many boys.

The incident was not really a telling-off and I think all of his rugby mates in the class saw this as just another funny incident. Keith himself saw the funny side of it afterwards and this added to his "street cred" anyway.

I didn't mean it to happen but from that day on Keith became known as "Porky", which I think still exists today.

Picture of Keith Lawrence

Picture of Keith follows (he is on the left). Also in the picture is Mark "Ty Mawr" Jones, holding the ball, who went on to play international rugby for Wales at senior level, gaining over 50 international caps.

Mark himself also had funny incidents, one of which also deserves mention.

Mark was a farmer's son and the family home was called "Ty Mawr", hence the nickname. He was an all-action lad and I could see from a very early age that he was destined for fame. Not only was he powerfully built, but he had electric acceleration and such was his agility, he could turn on a sixpence. His physical capability gave him tremendous confidence, but at the same time he was unassuming, although one day he met his match in a parent called Mrs Mary Morgan.

In school I acquired a "baby belling" cooker that was transported to each class for one day a week and parents were invited to come and take a group of children from that particular class for cooking.

Mark, at the time, was in Class 2. He was 7 years old. It was his turn for cooking and on this particular occasion Mrs Mary Morgan, a retired "no-nonsense nurse" and former parent, came into his class to take cooking.

Mark had just finished making his fairy cakes and was proudly showing them off and going back to his desk, when Mrs Morgan said to him, "Where do you think you are going, Mark?"

"I've finished," he said to Mrs Morgan.

"You haven't… Get back to the sink, clear up, and do the washing up… Get back here and tidy up."

I doubt he found anyone more combative in his illustrious international rugby career.

I was not exempt from the passion of parents. It was early in my days as head teacher, when I was confronted by a parent who clearly was unhappy about how things were shaping up at school when she confronted me at an open evening, pointing her finger at me and saying, "It's all your fault!"

Picture of confrontation

Momentarily I tried to recall any incidents during the week to which she might be referring. I naturally didn't want a confrontation in the school hall so I invited her into my office to discuss the matter.

She sat down, still clearly agitated and said, "My little Mary came home yesterday and I saw them crawling through her hair... Nits! We didn't have any before you came!"

Gathering my thoughts very quickly, relieved that it wasn't too serious, I explained to her that the new school with almost 100 children and growing all the time, was now nearly five times the size of her original village school and inevitably as more children gather there would be a much greater chance of getting nits!

She then realised that I had made a valid point, but still left in not too happy a mood!

CHAPTER 9

The Holistic Approach

Coming to this idyllic part of the country to live was a privilege, especially with its strong traditions of music and drama. It would be unforgivable not to capitalise on this to the benefit of the children, especially now the new school, with its vastly increased number of pupils, would enable music and drama to flourish in a more expansive way than in the individual schools.

Many of the children were from established farming families that had been in the area for generations, and had been immersed in the Eisteddfod tradition. The majority of the children also belonged to Young Farmers Clubs that regularly performed in dramas and singing events.

With this in mind it was obligatory to carry on this tradition in the school given the opportunity the new larger school afforded.

It was also important not only to marry them into one strong unit, but to continue healthy rivalry, which already existed in different Young Farmers Clubs, in the school, with "school houses" of Red, Blue, Yellow, and Green, each named after the local streams of:

Red: The Irfon
Blue: The Cammarch

Yellow: The Chwefru

Green: The Dulas

The school at the time was also very fortunate to have on staff a very musical and gifted nursery assistant who came with the staff from Beulah when it closed.

In my previous school in Swindon I was also given the opportunity by the head to direct one of the musical productions before I left. This clearly gave me the expertise and confidence to do the same at my own school.

However, for the first Christmas at the new school I thought it wise to just continue with a whole-school nativity.

From then on we had a traditional carol service but in addition, we launched into musical productions based on versions of all the classic musicals including: Oliver, Scrooge, Annie, The Wizard of Oz, Joseph, The Pied Piper, Hans Christian Andersen et al, always paying royalties for using the music to the appropriate authority.

The school hall also led itself beautifully for such by having a unique design feature – the staging could be stored in the floor and erected at the front of the hall, creating a well in the middle where part of the audience could be seated.

It was like an auditorium with two levels for the seating and an extra level at the front created by the staging out of the floor. It created a real theatre atmosphere and was such that all children could be seen from any position in the audience!

The following photographs come from just one of our productions. Our version of Scrooge.

There were no stage curtains and all scene changes had to be conducted during musical interludes or dimming the light to allow for scenery to be moved.

In addition, each scene was introduced by a narrator. Everything was planned to the second with no breaks in continuity. It was first rate and drew praise from the whole community.

It was policy that every child in class 4 would have an additional speaking part.

Class 3 children would have their individual opportunities the following year.

Pictures from Scrooge production

Preparations for the school production began early in October with all children eagerly waiting to find out what they would be involved in. All the songs were learnt by half term, fitting into the normal school routine.

Rehearsals for the main parts took place after half term, always at least three for every part in order that as many children as possible would have the opportunity to star.

At the same time the infant department were busily engaged in their own production for Christmas, with equal enthusiasm from the children.

By the end of November it was time to put the production together with dance routines and entrance/exit plans.

Our school motto was that "if it is worth doing it must be done well", which all children and staff embraced.

In the first week of December full-scale rehearsals started for the whole production, with the local OAPs invited as the audience to give added impetus before the three performances for the parents.

In the second week there were three school performances for parents, with one in the afternoon in between two evenings to ensure the children did not become over tired.

At this point I must pay tribute to the amazing musical ability of a particular member of staff who was certainly the lynchpin to the school's amazing productions through the whole of my time as head of the school. I am referring to Mrs Ionwen Davies, who is now the musical director of the very successful Builth Wells Ladies' Choir. Mrs Davies left the school shortly after I retired.

Pictures of Programme Covers from some of the many productions

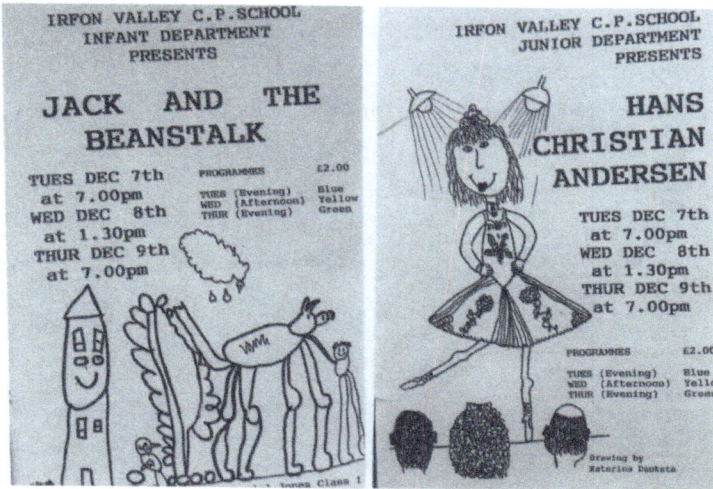

IRFON VALLEY C.P. SCHOOL
INFANT DEPARTMENT
PRESENTS

JACK AND THE BEANSTALK

TUES DEC 7th
at 7.00pm
WED DEC 8th
at 1.30pm
THUR DEC 9th
at 7.00pm

PROGRAMMES   £2.00
TUES (Evening)   Blue
WED (Afternoon) Yellow
THUR (Evening)   Green

IRFON VALLEY C.P. SCHOOL
JUNIOR DEPARTMENT
PRESENTS

HANS CHRISTIAN ANDERSEN

TUES DEC 7th
at 7.00pm
WED DEC 8th
at 1.30pm
THUR DEC 9th
at 7.00pm

PROGRAMMES   £2.00
TUES (Evening)   Blue
WED (Afternoon) Yellow
THUR (Evening)   Green

Videos were made of each performance with parental permission, which without exception was agreed and any parent wishing for a copy just paid for it to be made.

It gathered such praise that even the Director of Education came with his wife to see one of the performances.

Years later, in 1996, to the dismay of my parents, I was asked by the Local Authority as Chairman of the Small Rural Schools Committee (SRS) to lead the production of one of these musicals in the Wyeside Arts Theatre in Builth Wells, involving five other local schools.

It was a tremendous success, but such was the disappointment of my parents that our annual school production had been relocated to the Wyeside Arts Theatre in Builth Wells that I never repeated it!

Two other traditions were also introduced to the school routine to add to the development of the whole child, in the annual 3-day Educational Visit for all children in the top class, Yr. 5/6. The children spent two years in this class and during the autumn term of the first year they would have the opportunity to go on the London Visit, taking in all the sights and a West End musical production, and the following year they would be taken to an Adventure Centre in Mid Wales. In every case all children went without exception.

Pictures of annual outward bound visits

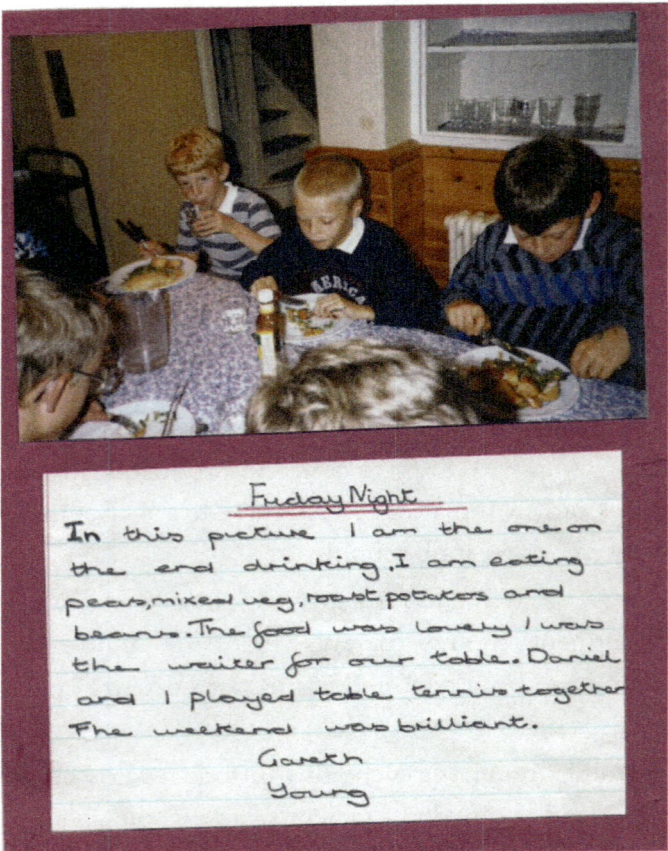

Friday Night

In this picture I am the one on the end drinking. I am eating peas, mixed veg, roast potatoes and beans. The food was lovely I was the waiter for our table. Daniel and I played table tennis together The weekend was brilliant.

Gareth
Young

Mining

It is Saturday morning and I am adjusting Daniel's helmet and light then he did the same for me. Everybody was in pairs. We were all excited because we didn't know what it was going to be like.

Gareth Young

Mining

In this picture we are actually in the mine. Chris Davies is carrying the ropes because if some of us were misbehaved John would tie us all together. John is throwing down a stone in a big hole. It took about 4 to 5 seconds to get to the bottom. He said the drops were above 250 feet deep.

Gareth Young

It was an excellent character-building exercise and all children eagerly awaited their opportunity.

Irfon Valley also had strong tradition in sport, especially in rugby, with the school winning the Powys Small Schools Tournament on numerous occasions in the 80s and 90s, producing players who went on to be professionals at the highest level.

Rugby success for Irfon Valley Boys

Six boys from Irfon Valley CP School, Builth Wells, have been chosen to represent Powys in the County Rugby Team. They are Ben Boucher, Gary Davies, Edward Protheroe, Gareth Nicholson, Michael Davies and Robert Kozak.

WIN FOR IRFON VALLEY At Talgarth on Tuesday 26th April Irfon Valley School won the South Powys Small Schools Rugby Tournament. In five games they only conceded one try and that was in the final against Mount Street 'B' side, Brecon. Leading try scorer for Irfon Valley was Robert Kozak who scored ten of the team's 11 tries. In four attempts since 1990 the school has won the trophy twice.

The Powys Small Schools Tournamen

The Powys Small Schools Tournamen

Mark "Ty Mawr" Jones, named after the family farm, went on to play for Wales over 50 times at senior level and then went on to be an international coach after knee injuries cut short his career.

Picture of Mark

Another lad, Lyndon Bateman, was an excellent back row forward who went on to play professional rugby for the Ospreys, one of the premier professional clubs in Wales.

Such was the enthusiasm for rugby that Rachel Davies, a little girl in class 4 who had a sparkling talent for all sports, became captain of one of our successful rugby teams, winning the Powys Schools Rugby Tournament, and went on to become an international player at under-16 level.

No boys complained at the time as she dictated the tactics – she was that good playing at scrum half.

Rachel's life, however, was tragically cut short at the age of nineteen when she was killed in a road crash travelling home from medical school in Manchester one Friday night.

Below is a picture of Rachel, captain of one of our winning school teams in the annual Powys County Rugby Championships.

Picture of Rachel as Captain of our winning team in the county tournament

I can still hear the cries of staff on yard duty shouting, "Get off that climbing frame before you hurt yourself, Rachel Davies!"

She was six or seven at the time. She was known as "Rach".

When we went to county swimming tournaments there was always a cry of anguish from other schools because she inspired other members of our team to win. She was also an incredible swimmer.

Irfon Valley won the county swimming tournament on numerous occasions with Rach in the team.

115

One other remarkable girl who went to Irfon Valley was Natalie Powell from Beulah, who was also multi-talented, and with enormous support from her parents decided that judo was for her, although so was so outstanding that anything was within her reach.

She was trained in Builth Wells Sports Centre at the local highly successful judo club and has gone on to be Commonwealth Champion.

Picture of Natalie

World Ranked Number 1 in 2017 (Britains first ever)
Double Olympian 2016 (7th) & 2021
World Championship Bronze Medalist Budapest 2017 (Wales's First ever)
3 x World Masters Medalist 2015, 2016, 2018
3 x European Championship Medalist 2016, 2017, 2018
Commonwealth Games Champion 2014 (Welsh Judo's first ever)
34 x World Tour medalist

Another lad quite gifted at all sports was David Young. who played badminton for Wales at secondary level, winning national titles and subsequently chosen to play for Wales at the Junior European Championships in Sofia in 1993.

Picture leaving for championship

There are so many who attended Irfon Valley during the 80s and 90s who went on to achieve at a high level in all walks of life, as well as many local children, now grown up, from farming families who have remained in the area and are the backbone of this community today; thoroughly grounded individuals and nice people.

I cannot conclude this chapter, however, without also mentioning two other members of staff who added so much to the life and welfare of the children in the school, giving them a firm foundation in life, helping in the school's approach of developing the "whole child" in our quest for "holistic" education.

Firstly I am referring to the school "cook in charge", Mrs Miriam Jones, known as MIM in the community. Mrs Jones was a formidable character, always immaculately turned out, as were her meals. Her kitchen, or inner sanctum, was only to be visited by appointment.

As well as the area where the children lined up for lunch, there was to the right a return hatch for used dinner plates. The hatch was large enough that a child could fit through and this was ideal as an additional entrance/exit during many of our Christmas productions.

For example: In "Hans Christian Andersen", the door to the cobbler's shop.

In "Oliver" it was the entrance to Fagan's den.

In "The Pied Piper" it was the entrance to the cave where the children were taken by the Pied Piper.

However, Mrs Jones and I had many interesting conversations about using her hatch as an entrance/exit for the above.

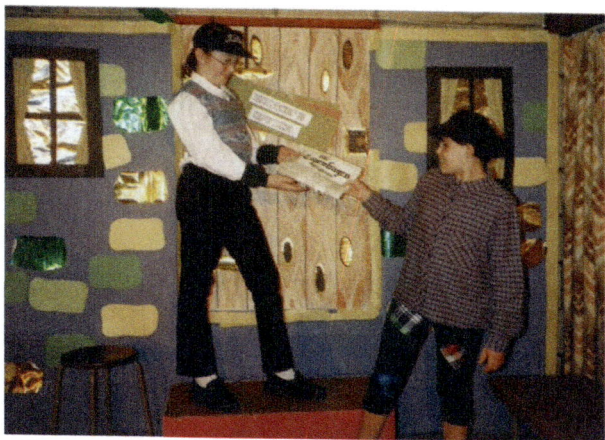

She did realise that the shows had to go on and I'm pleased to say that we always came to an amicable agreement!

The second member of staff that I must pay tribute to is my caretaker/cleaner. Mrs Mary Lawrence. The school's debt to her is immeasurable, as is my own. At the close of day we would spend time talking about any matters relating to the school cleaning, ensuring that any minor accidents with the décor were rectified.

While she had an allotted time for cleaning each evening she often overran this and would not leave until she was completely satisfied the school was like a new pin. She would rarely leave school before I did at 6.30 and I would go across the road with her to her home to have a cup of tea with her and "Den", her beloved husband, before I made my way home.

Mrs Lawrence would also come into school every Friday afternoon to undertake gardening with groups of children in our greenhouse, acquired out of school funds, bringing on flowers for the garden planters made by the children in class 4.

She never raised her voice and just a "look" was sufficient to remind any child how to behave, which was not very often as the children treated her as their favourite granny.

In 1995 the school had yet another very successful HM Inspection and during my follow-up meeting with the lead inspector I made special mention of Mrs Lawrence's contribution to the school and village life in general.

Shortly afterwards, Mrs Lawrence was awarded with an MBE.

Picture below of Mrs Lawrence receiving her MBE in Cardiff Castle presented by the then Prince of Wales

A little while before I retired I was walking around the school grounds during the dinner hour when I came across one of the infants crying bitterly. "Whatever is the matter?" I said to him.

"It's Woody… He's on the roof!"

It was about the time when "Toy Story" was all the rage with young children. He had been playing a game with Woody, throwing him up in the air, but he accidently threw him so high he went on the roof. I had no option but to get the long ladder out of the boiler room and climb up onto the roof to get Woody down.

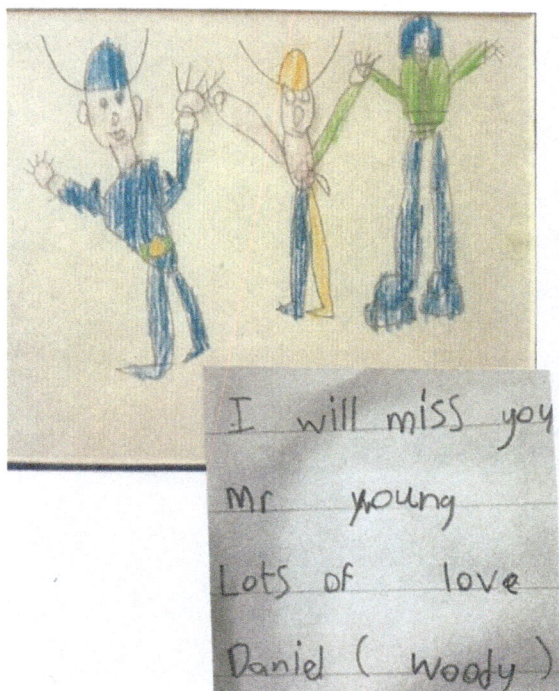

Woody picture

It was now 2001. The school was riding high and I was coming up to retirement age early in the following academic year, and so I felt it was the right time to allow the incoming head to have a full first year in post.

Finally, however, I must pay tribute to my first deputy head of Irfon Valley, Mrs Williams, the former head of old Garth School. She was truly the most professional and loyal colleague I have ever had the privilege to work with. She helped me in so many ways to establish the new school in the first five years. It was a very sad time for me when she retired.

My retirement picture

CHAPTER 10

Training the next generation of teachers

It was 6th Oct 2003 on a Saturday evening. The phone rang … my wife answered. "Could I speak to Mr Young, please? It is very important."

"Can I help you?" replied my wife.

"I'm afraid not."

"He's down the sports hall at the moment in a keep-fit class."

"Could you get him to ring me the minute he gets back?"

Minutes later my mobile pinged.

"Please come home soon, someone wants you rather urgently it seems."

As soon as I arrived I rang the number given to my wife.

"Mr Young, would you be interested in a position as a postgraduate primary science tutor/ lecturer for a teaching training establishment?"

To be honest I had previously been offered a similar position a little over a year earlier, but on that occasion I declined as I felt it was too soon after retirement and I needed to recharge my batteries... I hesitated for a moment and then I felt I could not refuse again, as the opportunity might never arise again!

"Yes, I would," I replied.

The response was immediate. "Good! In that case, could you start work this coming Monday? There are 75 postgraduate trainees in this year's cohort, some of whom will be starting out on a year-long course for the first time, while others are making a career change to pursue teaching. There are three groups of trainees, split into groups so that you will be taking 25 at a time for three-hour weekly sessions."

"As it happens," I said, "I am working for the Local Education Authority this coming Monday morning. However I could be available for a 1.30pm start."

"Unfortunately you would be taking two groups that afternoon, as you are not available for the morning session, and the third group the following morning..."

"Possible," I responded, "but not easy!"

The die was cast... I had always wanted to continue in Education and in this case it would involve my favourite subject... Science.

For the next 24 hours or so I frantically sorted material for this very important lecture. Fortunately I was given a "free hand" about the content.

I decided that it would have to have a practical element at the heart of it involving all the trainees from the very start to establish what I believe to be at the heart of sound practice in Education, and that is "direct involvement of students, making them the drivers and not passive recipients in the learning process".

Sadly for this first lecture, however, there would have to be compromise because with the best wish in the world I would not be able to gather enough equipment for everyone to pursue the work in an individually practical way.

I was determined, though, that everyone would be engaged in investigating an everyday occurrence that all children love to be involved in, especially at this time, when the weather was unusually cold and slippery underfoot.

After arriving from a mad dash from the north of the county I arrived just before 1.30pm. I started by introducing myself and then immediately delved into the daily lives and interests of children by posing a simple question about footwear and playground activities that children love to take part in…

"Sliding about in the playground when slippery underfoot!"

It was 2003 and the beginning of the age of oversupervision, of not allowing children a little freedom to enjoy themselves was rapidly receding just like the abolition of the "conker contest" for health and safety reasons.

I was on very safe ground (pun excused) as at this stage as I had not told any of the trainee Teachers exactly where this lecture was heading and I am sure they were all puzzled and thinking, *Is he really a Science Tutor/Lecturer or someone they just dragged in for the day?!*

They all breathed a sigh of relief though that they didn't immediately have a PowerPoint lecture thrust in front of them on an overhead screen to contend with!!

I continued the conversation about various items of footwear and asked them to look very closely at their own, and then tell me how safe they thought each one was. This was an immediate ploy to engage each trainee in direct observation.

I, however, had already taken notice of the trainees' footwear when they entered the lecture room.

At the heart of my lecture was going to be the importance of observation especially in scientific investigation, followed up with a **practical activity to prove or disprove their individual observations about the safety or otherwise of the footwear in slippery underfoot conditions**... in this case which item of footwear would be the safest.

The scene was set... No A-Level theory, no PowerPoint to drive everyone mad... just observation, discussion, and practical investigation.

After discussions amongst themselves I called everyone to order and invited a specially selected half-dozen students to bring me one shoe/boot, all having very different soles, and continued a discussion with everyone about their particular choice of footwear for that day and how safe they thought it to be for these underfoot conditions.

They were each given a simple recording sheet on a clipboard and asked to decide on a scale of 1 to 6 the safety of each, with 1 being the safest and 6 being the most unsafe in the prevailing conditions.

Recording sheet:

Safety under foot during poor weather conditions.

Footwear	Safety prediction 1-6 (1. safest)	Actual Result
A		
B		
C		
D		

The overall prediction as seen from their result papers was that **"footwear with the deepest treads would be safest to wear!"**

All sheets were filled in. Now the practical work began, but first their hypothesis had to be put to the test.

Just as in a classroom situation, they were challenged to think about how their theory could be put to the test indoors. A practical situation would have to be set up so that each item of footwear could be tested under the same conditions... In other words **creating a fair test under laboratory conditions.**

The trainees were now fully engaged in something that they all had experience in... **a real-life problem without any fear of being humiliated or feeling silly for saying something.**

It is surprising that in this situation with a little gentle encouragement ideas start to flow, with everyone wishing to say something. It seemed obvious that as we could not create the icy, slippery surface in the comfort of the lecture room another avenue had to be pursued involving the treads of the footwear, to see which one would grip best.

Again, after almost no time at all one trainee said, **"Why don't we produce a slope and see which grips the surface best?"**

Without realising it they were actually constructing their own **"fair testing"** situation, applied to the footwear. A basic skill to be developed in children.

The next part of this problem situation now had to be solved... What apparatus would be needed and how would the footwear be measured in terms of grip?

Again discussion followed and it was decided that we needed a surface upon which the shoes could be placed that could be tilted in equal intervals until the shoes moved down the slope without stopping.

At the same time, on this occasion I produced a metre length of MDF board for this purpose and a half-dozen 4x2-inch blocks of wood. I asked the trainees to consider the potential age of the children to be challenged with this problem, and how this would impact on deciding what method they would use to determine the result. Clearly Key Stage 1 children's measuring strategy would be far less involved than Key Stage 2. After further discussion we decided the board would be tilted one block at a time and the number of blocks used for each shoe/boot would determine the result.

Picture of Practical investigation for Key Stage 1 (5-7 year olds)...
Friction

This would be a satisfying method for Key Stage 1 (infant children) but if repeated with Key Stage 2 (junior children) a more sophisticated method would be used involving a large classroom protractor to measure the slope in degrees.

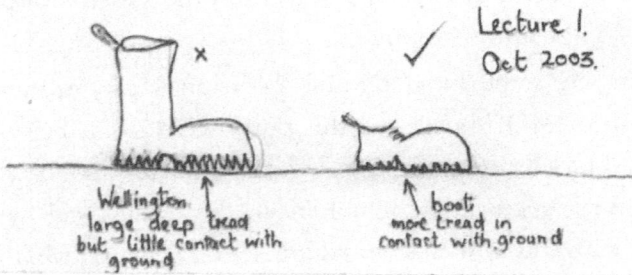

Picture using a large classroom protractor for Key Stage 2 children

Clearly it was important to discuss this differentiation as some trainees had opted to teach Key Stage 1 children while others wanted to take up a position once trained with older Key Stage 2 children.

The lecture was scheduled for three hours and the time was used to obtain a result that to many, was totally surprising, and it opened their eyes to the need for them and children to be actively engaged in finding solutions to everyday occurrences. It proved that children should be active participants and not passive recipients in the learning process. Overwhelmingly this practical investigation, in which everyone was totally absorbed, demonstrated that the amount of surface contact the footwear has with the ground is the deciding factor, and not the depth of tread.

Friction between surfaces increases with the amount of surface in contact with each other.

MORE surface contact, more friction, more grip.

First lecture… complete success with everyone looking forward to the next!!!

I repeated the same lecture to the third group the following morning.

Before I left the lecture room that day, however, I discussed how this could be put into practice with a complete class of 25-30 children – not uncommon!! Six specially cut lengths of MDF board would be used, each measuring 1m by 25cm, and a number of 4x2in wooden blocks, available from any builder's yard. Each board would serve as a base board for the investigation. It would serve them for their whole teaching career without scrabbling for apparatus the next day, week, month, term, or whatever!

This should be housed in their practical equipment resource box ready for next time!

Teaching is not rocket science, but really about preparation.

After this initial success I had to create a complete Science module for a year-long postgraduate course for 75 trainee teachers in Core Science! This was both a frightening and exhilarating thought. The preparation started immediately but it did not happen overnight. The whole of the first year was a week-by-week affair with me assembling practical apparatus I had used successfully used over decades with children, comprising in the main of bits and bobs of discarded household material used in everyday life. Successful Primary Science is driven by practical investigation involving all the children.

Each week of the first year I took a different aspect of Science, making it into a practical problem-solving situation for the trainees, as if they were the children they would be confronted with in little less than a year's time on a daily basis!

Each week the format of my lecture was the same:

A brief introduction talking about an everyday situation that children might encounter and then a discussion as to how to solve it.

The trainees were split into 6 groups of 4 usually **so that all were engaged in first-hand activity.**

Each week I took a different area of Science to produce a 3hr package of work.

I recorded this in the weekly copy of *Keynotes*, the university publication available for the trainees each week. The useful offshoot of this was to consolidate the previous week's lecture.

Examples of these contributions follow, including pictures taken during the lecture.

Title: How to stop Goldilocks from breaking into the house of the three bears!

In a previous lecture the trainees had already revised their understanding of simple electrical circuits using a 1.5v bulb, battery, and plastic-coated wire, so this lecture was a natural follow-on.

We used shoe boxes for the house of the three bears, and made simple switches using folded card and silver foil.

Below are pictures from the session. Please note the smiles of satisfaction on the faces of the trainees – they come from interest, challenge, and practical involvement giving ownership and understanding. That's what teaching is all about!!

Harry Young: Early Years/Primary Science Subject Tutor

Burglar alarm pictures

Bringing Science to Life at the Half-Term Residential

Once a year the trainees attended a weekend residential course and I was also in attendance as the Core Science Tutor.

At this particular course, as one of my practical sessions I looked at the development of the wheel starting from the simple raft many thousands of years ago.

Below are pictures from the practical session. As you can see, it is not deskbound note taking from a PowerPoint session!

Development of the wheel pictures

Bridge the gap!

In this session I challenged the trainees to make me the strongest bridge possible from a single sheet of A4 cartridge paper. No scissors were allowed: the only option was to fold the paper.

They were given two 4x2 wooden blocks and told to bridge a gap 20cm wide. Note their efforts. They were split into small groups ensuring complete "first hand" investigation. No computer simulation!

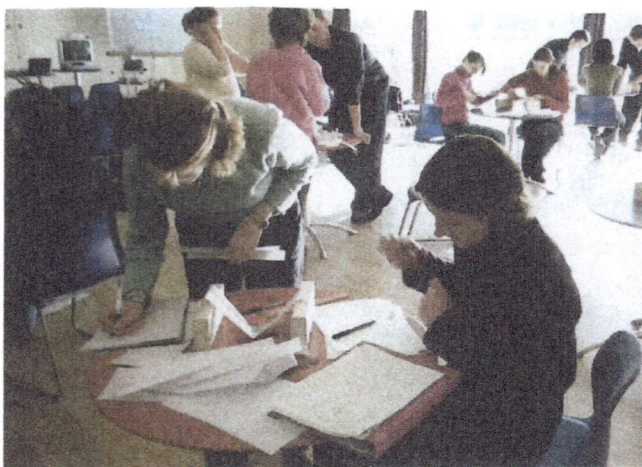

Bridging the gap pictures

In my position as the Core Science adviser/tutor for the Early Years Primary Science Course from 2003 to 2013/4, I was involved in a number of HM Inspections.

Below are excerpts from the 2013 HM Inspection relating to Primary Science:

"Centre-based training is of high quality. The content is extensive and there is a strong emphasis on practical learning. Trainees are given a wealth of resources and practical ideas that are applicable to the continuum across the Early Years Foundation Stage and both primary key stages. Trainees express very high levels of satisfaction with this component of their training."

At a number of Graduation Ceremonies I was awarded with the Co-operative Teacher Trainer Award of the year and below is a picture of me going to receive my award in 2009 at the graduation ceremony.

Tutor of the Year Award 2013

Finally and sadly, it all came to an end in 2014 when the Government introduced the "Schools Direct" programme, where postgrads were no longer required to have a year's centre-based training to achieve QTS (Qualified Teacher Status) but went immediately into schools to train on the job!

As a result establishments such as the one in which I was employed closed. It was always difficult to recruit teachers anyway as it was never a 9 to 3pm occupation, as many thought.

Society at large has changed beyond recognition as parents spend less time with their children for a variety of reasons, and this breakdown in family life is causing catastrophic consequences for children.

Education is a triangle of learning with the child at the apex and school and home forming the base. If home and/or school fail, the child will suffer.

Triangle of learning picture

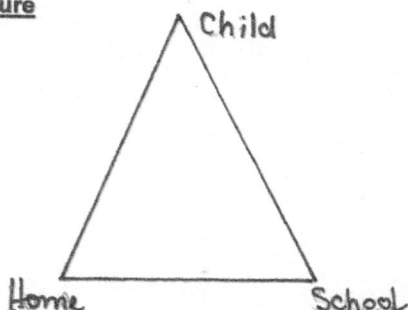

In schools there is an ever-increasing pressure and reliance on IT to drive forward education with little input from the child, other than to press the appropriate key on the computer. This way forward, without interaction of fellow pupils, is detrimental to producing well-rounded children able to interact with their peers.

IT has a vital and increasingly important role to play in education for information seeking, which saves vital time in the learning process, but it should be an aid, not a replacement to learning per se. The basics of Numeracy/Literacy have never been more important than at the present time.

I believe the child should be at the centre of the learning process where "simple hands-on investigation" of the world around them, with interaction of fellow pupils, is the best way to produce well-rounded individuals in the future.

However, there must be optimism in that there are always passionate young people coming through to take up the challenge of teaching!

My time has come to an end... perhaps! I feel very proud and privileged to have been part of the lives of so many children and young adults over such a long period of time!

Over the years I have been sent many messages of thanks by former pupils and trainees.

Below are cards given to me that I feel sum it all up and have made my journey worthwhile.

When Harry met PGCE Primary

There's a Science Teacher - Young is his name
Once you have met him - your life's never quite the same

His jokes, his laughter - you can't ignore
His sense of fun - you just have to adore

Harry has some fabulous facts and ingenious ideas to share
He's patient, flexible, enthusiastic - he really does care!

He told us to aim high - for the brightest star
But Harry - you are the shining example - by far!

You ignited our interest and showed us the way
To be great teachers like you at the end of the day

Harry - don't ever change - stay just as you are
Funny, imaginative and a bright shining star!

An original ode by Fiona McCall
July 2008 - on behalf of everyone
In the class of 07/08

Glossary of Education Terminology and Science based Definitions

Chapter 1 It doesn't have to work to be Successful

Density = mass/ Volume

Theory: 1 mil.(cc) of water has a mass of 1 gm. Anything that has a mass of less than 1 gm per 1 cubic cm of material will float on water because it is less dense but anything with a mass of more than 1 gm per cubic cm will sink....QED

In other words if the mass of the material is more than 1 gm per cubic cm it will sink as it is more dense than water and will not be supported on the surface of the water

Example: steel has a mass of .....7.8 gm per cc and so the density is 7.8

Because Density = Mass/Volume

$$7.8 = 7.8/1 (1 \text{ being the mass of 1 cc of water})$$

Chapter 2. I hear, I forget, I do I understand

Mechanical Advantage = Load/Effort

Velocity Ratio = Distance travelled by the effort/ Distance travelled by the load

Chapter 6. The Whole School Experience

The National Curriculum

With the formal introduction of the National Curriculum in the late Eighties particularly in Science came the introduction of the study areas in relation to Science known as:

ATs(attainment targets) which indicated the key areas to be taught*

Sc1: Investigative procedures

Sc2. Plants/Animals/Humans

Sc3. Materials

Sc4 Physical Processes (light, sound, electricity)

FINAL NOTE

I have been very fortunate in that I have experienced Education from the early 1940s as a pupil, right through the 50s until I trained to be a teacher at the start of the 60s and then have been immersed in Education ever since

The Educational pendulum has changed numerous times over the last 60 years from a tightly controlled curriculum to anything goes and back again, so much so, that all continuity is lost. What is clear is that extremes have no place in Education.

All children need to be taught the basics (3Rs) and once mastered need to use these skills in a wider context where the children themselves are placed at the centre of the learning process.

For this purpose, a few years ago after finally retiring, I created a website comprising a series of 8/10 minute videos made at my kitchen table.

The website has three main aims:
1. To provide practical ideas for the hard pressed primary school teacher to engage the children in simple "hands on" activities to make sense of the world around them.
2. To advise on easily obtainable equipment that can be used time after time for "whole class" participation.
3. To advise teachers on ways to link all practical work to the ever changing NC (National Curriculum) requirements

using the real situations in their environment as a starting point.

The website is:

practicalprimaryscience.co.uk

It can also be accessed on:

educationisnotrocketscience.co.uk

"Education is not Rocket Science" it is just about adopting a common sense approach!

ABOUT THE AUTHOR

I am married with two married sons. For nearly 60 years I have been working in the Education System in England and Wales. My career started in a secondary school as a science teacher in Newport, South Wales, in 1964, then after several years I moved on to teaching at primary school level in England.

I steadily gained experience at this level, becoming a Deputy Head Teacher of a very large junior school before returning to Wales appointed as a Head Teacher of a new purpose-built area community primary school following the closure of five small village schools.

I remained there in post for over 20 years, retiring at 60. The calling of education, however, was still strong, and I was invited to return as a Postgraduate Lecturer for science for those wishing to attain PGCE status to teach in the Primary Sector, finally retiring at the age of 73.

I was an active participant in sport, playing rugby throughout the sixties, privileged to play against some of the finest teams in England and Wales at this time. After retirement I turned to squash and golf, however, my favourite leisure-time activity is fly fishing.

In recent years I now also have developed a love for painting local scenes in watercolour and acrylic. In addition, for the last ten years I have returned to motorcycle riding through the beautiful countryside of rural mid-Wales.

Printed in Great Britain
by Amazon